"MY RARE WIT KILLING SIN"

The Other Voice in Early Modern Europe: The Toronto Series, 27

The Other Voice in
Early Modern Europe:
The Toronto Series

Previous Publications in the Series

MADRE MARÍA ROSA
Journey of Five Capuchin Nuns
Edited and translated by Sarah E. Owens
2009

GIOVAN BATTISTA ANDREINI
Love in the Mirror: A Bilingual Edition
Edited and translated by Jon R. Snyder
2009

RAYMOND DE SABANAC AND SIMONE ZANACCHI
Two Women of the Great Schism: The Revelations *of Constance de Rabastens by Raymond de Sabanac and* Life of the Blessed Ursulina of Parma *by Simone Zanacchi*
Edited and translated by Renate Blumenfeld-Kosinski and Bruce L. Venarde
2010

OLIVA SABUCO DE NANTES BARRERA
The True Medicine
Edited and translated by Gianna Pomata
2010

LOUISE-GENEVIÈVE GILLOT DE SAINCTONGE
Dramatizing Dido, Circe, and Griselda
Edited and translated by Janet Levarie Smarr
2010

PERNETTE DU GUILLET
Complete Poems: A Bilingual Edition
Edited by Karen Simroth James
Translated by Marta Rijn Finch
2010

ANTONIA PULCI
Saints' Lives and Bible Stories for the Stage: A Bilingual Edition
Edited by Elissa B. Weaver
Translated by James Wyatt Cook
2010

VALERIA MIANI
Celinda, A Tragedy: A Bilingual Edition
Edited by Valeria Finucci
Translated by Julia Kisacky
Annotated by Valeria Finucci and Julia Kisacky
2010

Enchanted Eloquence: Fairy Tales by Seventeenth-Century French Women Writers
Edited and translated by Lewis C. Seifert and Domna C. Stanton
2010

GOTTFRIED WILHELM LEIBNIZ, SOPHIE, ELECTRESS OF HANOVER AND QUEEN SOPHIE CHARLOTTE OF PRUSSIA
Leibniz and the Two Sophies: The Philosophical Correspondence
Edited and translated by Lloyd Strickland
2011

The Other Voice in Early Modern Europe: The Toronto Series

Previous Publications in the Series

In Dialogue with the Other Voice in Sixteenth-Century Italy: Literary and Social Contexts for Women's Writing
Edited by Julie D. Campbell and Maria Galli Stampino
2011

SISTER GIUSTINA NICCOLINI
The Chronicle of Le Murate
Edited and translated by Saundra Weddle
2011

LIUBOV KRICHEVSKAYA
No Good without Reward: Selected Writings: A Bilingual Edition
Edited and translated by Brian James Baer
2011

ELIZABETH COOKE HOBY RUSSELL
The Writings of an English Sappho
Edited by Patricia Phillippy
With translations by Jaime Goodrich
2011

LUCREZIA MARINELLA
Exhortations to Women and to Others if They Please
Edited and translated by Laura Benedetti
2012

MARGHERITA DATINI
Letters to Francesco Datini
Translated by Carolyn James and Antonio Pagliaro
2012

DELARIVIER MANLEY AND MARY PIX
English Women Staging Islam, 1696–1707
Edited and introduced by Bernadette Andrea
2012

CECILIA DEL NACIMIENTO
Journeys of a Mystic Soul in Poetry and Prose
Introduction and prose translations by Kevin Donnelly
Poetry translations by Sandra Sider
2012

LADY MARGARET DOUGLAS AND OTHERS
The Devonshire Manuscript: A Women's Book of Courtly Poetry
Edited and introduced by Elizabeth Heale
2012

ARCANGELA TARABOTTI
Letters Familiar and Formal
Edited and translated by Meredith K. Ray and Lynn Lara Westwater
2012

The Other Voice in
Early Modern Europe:
The Toronto Series

SERIES EDITORS Margaret L. King *and* Albert Rabil, Jr.
SERIES EDITOR, ENGLISH TEXTS Elizabeth H. Hageman

Previous Publications in the Series

PERE TORRELLAS AND JUAN DE FLORES
Three Spanish Querelle *Texts:* Grisel and Mirabella, The Slander against Women, *and* The Defense of Ladies against Slanderers*: A Bilingual Edition and Study*
Edited and translated by Emily C. Francomano
2013

BARBARA TORELLI BENEDETTI
Partenia, a Pastoral Play: A Bilingual Edition
Edited and translated by Lisa Sampson and Barbara Burgess-Van Aken
2013

FRANÇOIS ROUSSET, JEAN LIEBAULT, JACQUES GUILLEMEAU, JACQUES DUVAL AND LOUIS DE SERRES
Pregnancy and Birth in Early Modern France: Treatises by Caring Physicians and Surgeons (1581–1625)
Edited and translated by Valerie Worth-Stylianou
2013

MARY ASTELL
The Christian Religion, as Professed by a Daughter of the Church of England
Edited by Jacqueline Broad
2013

SOPHIA OF HANOVER
Memoirs (1630–1680)
Edited and translated by Sean Ward
2013

KATHERINE AUSTEN
Book M: A London Widow's Life Writings
Edited by Pamela S. Hammons
2013

"My Rare Wit Killing Sin": Poems of a Restoration Courtier

ANNE KILLIGREW

~

Edited by

MARGARET J. M. EZELL

Iter Inc.
Centre for Reformation and Renaissance Studies
Toronto
2013

Iter: Gateway to the Middle Ages and Renaissance
Tel: 416/978–7074 Email: iter@utoronto.ca
Fax: 416/978–1668 Web: www.itergateway.org

Centre for Reformation and Renaissance Studies
Victoria University in the University of Toronto
Tel: 416/585–4465 Email: crrs.publications@utoronto.ca
Fax: 416/585–4430 Web: www.crrs.ca

Printed in Canada.

Iter and the Centre for Reformation and Renaissance Studies gratefully acknowledge the generous support of James E. Rabil, in memory of Scottie W. Rabil, toward the publication of this book.

Library and Archives Canada Cataloguing in Publication
Killigrew, Anne, 1660–1685
[Poems]
"My rare wit killing sin": poems of a Restoration courtier / Anne Killigrew ; edited by Margaret J. M. Ezell.
(Other voice in early modern Europe. Toronto series ; 27)
Modernized version of the work Killigrew, Anne, 1660–1685. Poems, published in London by Samuel Lowndes in 1686.
Includes bibliographical references and indexes.
Issued in print and electronic formats.
Co-published by: Iter Inc.

ISBN 978-0-7727-2152-5 (pbk.)
ISBN 978-0-7727-2153-2 (pdf)

I. Ezell, Margaret J. M., writer of introduction, editor II. Victoria University (Toronto, Ont.). Centre for Reformation and Renaissance Studies, issuing body III. Iter Inc., issuing body IV. Title. V. Series: Other voice in early modern Europe. Toronto series ; 27

PR3539.K3 2013 821'.4 C2013-907241-1
C2013-907242-X

Cover illustration: *Anne Killigrew* (mezzotint engraving), by Isaac Beckett, after Anne Killigrew self-portrait; published by John Smith, c. 1683–1729; © National Portrait Gallery, London, NPG D11896.

Cover design:
Maureen Morin, Information Technology Services, University of Toronto Libraries.

Typesetting and production:
Iter Inc.

Contents

Illustrations

Cover Illustration. *Anne Killigrew* (mezzotint engraving), by Isaac Beckett, after Anne Killigrew self-portrait; published by John Smith, c. 1683–1729; © National Portrait Gallery, London, NPG D11896.

Plate 1. *Venus Attired by the Graces* (oil on canvas), Killigrew, Anne (c. 1660–c. 1685) / Private Collection / Photo © Philip Mould Ltd, London / The Bridgeman Art Library, MOU 316404.

Abbreviations

ODNB	*Oxford Dictionary of National Biography* (Online version)
OED	*Oxford English Dictionary* (Online Version)

Acknowledgments

Many thanks first go to my student assistants at Texas A&M University, Soha Chung and Elizabeth Brandeberry, for their help in preparing this volume. Their suggestions and painstaking attention to detail made working on this edition a rewarding experience for all of us. My thanks also go to my former student Michael Rex, whose early thesis on Killigrew drew attention to Killigrew's epic heroines. My research on Killigrew was supported by funding from the Sara and John Lindsey Chair of Liberal Arts at Texas A&M University. I also am grateful for the insights on Killigrew and the court of Mary of Modena generously shared by James Winn and David Hopkins. Dr. Karin Kyburz at the Courtauld Institute of Art offered assistance concerning the whereabouts of Killigrew's portraits. David Smith and Eleanor Taylor at Berkeley Castle patiently answered my questions about the Anne Killigrew paintings in that collection. Suzanne Nicholls at the Hertfordshire Archives and Local Studies Centre answered several queries confirming genealogical records relating to Anne Killigrew's sisters. My husband, Lawrence Griffing, assisted me in tracking down several of Killigrew's paintings and documenting their whereabouts, as well as preparing the manuscript for publication. I am also grateful to the Brotherton Collection at the University of Leeds for permission to publish Edmund Wodehouse's poem on Killigrew and to Ruth Lightbourne, Curator of Rare Books at the Alexander Turnbull Library, for providing photographs of the manuscript of Edmond Elys's verses. The self-portrait of Killigrew that served as the frontispiece for her 1686 volume is reproduced here courtesy of National Portrait Gallery, London, with thanks to Emma Butterfield for her assistance; the illustration of Killigrew's painting *Venus Attired by the Graces* is reproduced with the permission of Bridgeman Art Library International.

Finally, this volume is dedicated with affection and respect to Elizabeth H. Hageman, who has spent a career making sure that other voices can be clearly heard and to letting other students and scholars share in the fun and excitement of finding and reading them.

Plate 1. *Venus Attired by the Graces* (oil on canvas), Killigrew, Anne (c.1660–c.1685) / Private Collection / Photo © Philip Mould Ltd, London / The Bridgeman Art Library.

Introduction

The Other Voice

"My rare wit killing sin."
—Edmund Wodehouse, "Anagram on Mistress Anne Killigrew"[1]

Anne Killigrew (1660–1685) spoke through multiple voices: her own voice as she expressed herself through her poetry; the public voice created for her by her grieving father who printed an edition of the manuscript verses by her and others found in her possession after her death; and the iconic voice constructed for her by poets commenting on her life and writings, most prominently and influentially, the poet laureate John Dryden. This volume, while preserving the representation of Killigrew by others, seeks to highlight her individual voice—that of a young, single woman closely associated with the Restoration courts of both King Charles II and his wife Queen Catherine and of James, Duke of York, the future James II, and his second wife, Mary of Modena. Yet, as the anagram made on her name by Edmund Wodehouse suggests, Anne Killigrew gazed thoughtfully on the fashionable world she was born into and, in her life and poetry, rejected its values.

When one thinks of the Restoration period and in particular of the culture of the courts of King Charles II and his brother James, Duke of York, the most common association is with the hedonistic, libertine life-style followed by many of both the male courtiers and the women associated with them. The notorious rake John Wilmot, Earl of Rochester, had passed away from syphilis in 1680 at age thirty-three, five years before Killigrew herself would die from smallpox. Wilmot and others in their satiric verses created scathing portraits of the women of the court as scheming their way to fortune and titles through their publicly acknowledged affairs. Charles and James both openly maintained their mistresses and illegitimate children. Barbara Palmer, Countess of Castlemaine, who was Charles II's most powerful mistress, commented sardonically about the general atmosphere of the

1. University of Leeds, Brotherton Library, MS Lt 40, fol. 124v.

court that her young daughter by the king, Charlotte Fitzroy, who was betrothed at ten and married at twelve, would be the only true "maid" on her wedding day of all the so-called "maids of honor" serving the royal households.[2] Traditional literary histories of the period that rely on the contemporary satires and lampoons in circulation have also depicted the young women in the courts as being intent on securing a fortune and a titled husband and thus available for the attentions of the royal brothers and their courtiers; they have also tended to focus on the writings of the so-called "court wits," the male poets and dramatists who entertained Charles with their writings extolling sexual conquest and aggressively challenging the institutions of family and religion in their plays, poems, and in their own libertine behavior.

Through an extensive network of family relations, Anne Killigrew was closely tied to these courts and was, like many of her female relatives, a maid of honor, serving in the court of the Duke of York's wife, Mary of Modena.[3] She was also an artist, painting the portraits of James, Mary, and members of their courts, as well as self-portraits.[4] While living in this milieu, Anne Killigrew was also writing about amazon warrior queens, heroic wives, and about rejecting social customs that seemed to demand that young people of both sexes be mercenary predators. Hers is the other voice of Restoration court culture: female, ambitiously literary, and in opposition to the prevailing libertine ethos

2. Samuel Pepys, *The Diary of Samuel Pepys*, ed. Phil Gyford, based on Henry B. Wheatley, ed., *The Diary of Samuel Pepys*, 9 vols. (London, 1893), diary entry February 21, 1665 at http://www. pepysdiary.com/archive/1665/02/. All subsequent references to Pepys's diary are to this website by the date of the entry.

3. There has been some dispute among critics writing on Killigrew in recent years over whether or not she actually served as a maid of honor; the most recent entry on her in the *Oxford Dictionary of National Biography*, however, now states unequivocally that she does appear on the list of maids of honor in 1683. David Hopkins, "Killigrew, Anne (1660–1685)," *Oxford Dictionary of National Biography*, ed. Lawrence Goldman (Oxford: Oxford University Press, 2004–), (accessed July 10, 2012) at http://www. oxforddnb. com. All subsequent references to the *ODNB* are to the online edition.

4. Carol Barash, *English Women's Poetry, 1649–1714: Politics, Community, and Linguistic Authority* (Oxford: Oxford University Press, 1996), 159. In a private communication, James Winn has also pointed to the facial resemblances of the figures in Killigrew's painting *Venus Attired by the Graces* as being like those in other portraits of Anne Finch, Mary of Modena, and Anne Killigrew herself.

of the court. A contemporary of hers who also was a maid of honor in the court of Mary of Modena, Anne Finch, Countess of Winchilsea, declared later that she never engaged in literary pursuits while at the court because she feared being labeled a "versifying maid of honor" and the social scorn that might bring.[5] Anne Killigrew, as seen in the body of work she left behind, was eager to write poetry that would bring her what she considered to be true and lasting fame.

Restoration England: History, Politics, and Religion

The exact day of Anne Killigrew's birth is unknown, but we do know that she was born in 1660, just as the restoration of the monarchy to the throne of England was beginning. On May 29, 1660, on his thirtieth birthday, King Charles II rode through the streets of London in triumph after a long absence. He had been in exile in Europe after the execution of his father Charles I by Parliament in January 1649 during the English Civil Wars and his own subsequent defeat as he attempted to invade through Scotland in 1651 to retake the country. Although the Restoration period is sometimes studied as being a clean break from the old style monarchy of Charles I and the subsequent Puritan rule during the Commonwealth, many of the key issues that affected the life of the court and its courtiers during the first two decades of the Restoration are continuations of old arguments and divisions, and many of the influential writers, artists, and politicians shaping the "new" Restoration were in fact born during the older regimes.

In the 1650s, the country initially was governed by Parliament and became a Commonwealth, but the Parliamentary general Oliver Cromwell soon gained complete control over the government and dismissed Parliament, ruling alone as Lord Protector. Many English Protestants at that time believed that the second coming of Christ was eminent, and that the civil wars had been a sign: England must prepare for the millennium by becoming a godly country, a nation of saints. Numerous edicts were passed during the 1650s banning frivolous activities that distracted from godly devotions, such as the publica-

5. Anne Finch, *The Poems of Anne, Countess of Winchilsea*, ed. Myra Reynolds (Chicago: University of Chicago Press, 1903), 7–8.

tion of "merry books" and sporting events such as horse racing.[6] The London theaters, which had been officially closed in 1642, struggled to exist with clandestine performances, frequently raided by the army, with both its actors and the audiences facing fines and imprisonment. The celebration of Christmas was banned as a pagan festival, and even daily language was purified, with pagan words for days of the week and names of months being frequently replaced by numbers, as seen in the title of an entertainment by William Davenant, *The First Day's Entertainment at Rutledge House* performed in 1656. Davenant (1606–1668) had been a favorite dramatist of Queen Henrietta Maria before the war for his platonic comedies and his masque *The Temple of Love* (1635) written to be performed by the queen and her ladies in waiting. During the Commonwealth, he offered Cromwell and his Puritan audience instead of pastoral romance a series of staged debates over topics such as the value of public entertainments between two classical philosophers and a Parisian and a Londoner arguing for the virtues of each city.[7]

However, following the death of Cromwell in 1658, the Commonwealth government of England, Scotland, and Ireland fell quickly into factions and disarray. Oliver Cromwell's son Richard, who had succeeded him, was forced to abdicate, and the army led by General Monck marched on London to regain control. With the army in possession, Royalist sympathizers joined with remaining members of the recalled Parliament to request the return of King Charles II to restore not only the monarchy but also the national Church of England, or the Anglican Church, and the House of Lords.

Conflicts over matters of religious belief and practice which had sprung up during the civil war years and Commonwealth period continued after the Restoration between not only the increasingly visible number of Catholic aristocrats serving in positions of importance, raising the same fears that had in part triggered the civil wars, but also between the established Anglican Church of England and Protestant denominations such as the Baptists and Presbyterians, and the more

6. Margaret J. M. Ezell, "Never Boring, or Imagine My Surprise: Interregnum Woman and the Culture of Reading," in *Imagining Selves: Essays in Honor of Patricia Meyer Spacks*, ed. Rivka Swenson and Elise Lauterbach (Newark: University of Delaware Press, 2008), 155–69.

7. Mary Edmond, "Davenant, Sir William (1606–1668)," *ODNB*.

radical groups such as the Quakers. These very different groups are referred to during the 1660s as "nonconformists" because they refused to take the required oaths required of those serving as public ministers under a series of laws passed by Parliament known as The Clarendon Code (1661–1665). This often resulted in these ministers being removed from their positions and even, like the Baptist preacher and author of *Pilgrim's Progress* (1678) John Bunyan, imprisoned for illegal preaching. The Killigrew family remained solidly within the Anglican Church and its hierarchy, although Anne's father Henry and her brothers-in-law were the family's only ministers, the other Killigrews apparently adhering to the pragmatic religion of the times and of the court.

The man whom General Monck and Parliament invited back to reclaim the throne of his father had been living the life of a defeated king with loyal followers but without a throne or power for over a decade. Charles, his brothers James and Henry, his sister Henrietta, and their mother Queen Henrietta Maria, resided mostly in France. Other royalist exiles were scattered about the Continent, many in the Netherlands. For the most part, the remaining royal family and many of the cavaliers with their own families who had followed them into exile, such as the Duke of Newcastle, William Cavendish and his wife, the prolific author Margaret Cavendish, spent the time living in near poverty, as Charles tried unsuccessfully to raise sufficient funds to support a military invasion of England to retake his throne. James, the younger brother, was able to enter the French army, where he served with distinction under General Turenne; later, along with his younger brother Henry, he joined the Spanish army. Anne Killigrew's father, Henry Killigrew, had been ordained as a minister in the Anglican Church as the war began; he had served as James's chaplain since 1642, following him into exile and eventually acting as a member of his cabinet council in Paris and Brussels. Charles, as the king of England albeit without a throne, could not follow this military path; he spent the first part of the decade with his mother in the palace at the Louvre in Paris, living off a small allowance granted by the French monarchy to her, and when that became too strained, he moved his court first to Bruges and then Brussels.

While in exile Charles had his first illegitimate child, a son with Lucy Walter in 1649. The boy was given the name James Crofts, but he was always acknowledged by Charles. After the Restoration, Charles raised him at court, giving him the title of the Duke of Monmouth and arranging a marriage for him with a wealthy young heiress, as well as providing him with a sizeable income through gifts and positions.[8] In later years, however, Charles flatly refused to endorse the widely circulated rumor that he had secretly wed Lucy Walter, which would have made Monmouth a legitimate Protestant heir to the throne. This would become increasingly a concern in the late 1670s and early 1680s when Anne Killigrew was growing up: Charles did not have any children with his queen, Catherine of Braganza, and there was widespread concern over his brother James, Duke of York, who had converted to Catholicism, succeeding to the throne.

While Charles was still in exile on the Continent, Monmouth's mother, Lucy Walter, was succeeded in Charles's affections by Anne Killigrew's aunt, Elizabeth Boyle, who gave birth to Charles's daughter in 1651, Charlotte Jemima. More affairs followed, and at least two more children were born out of wedlock while Charles was in exile. This pattern continued on Charles's return to England. Barbara Palmer, Countess of Castlemaine bore a child to him every year from 1661 to 1665; when Charles married the Portuguese Catholic princess Catherine of Braganza in May of 1662, he insisted that she accept Castlemaine as a lady of the bedchamber, which was a highly prestigious position in court. In the early 1660s, he pursued several of his wife's maids of honor, the most notable being Frances Stewart, who was the daughter of Queen Henrietta Maria's physician; the king was ardently and openly in love with her, but apparently without success, although to the scandal of observers. The irony of the gap between his own libertine behavior and the antics of his court and Charles's position as the head of the Church of England was not lost on observers. There was more tolerance of his affairs with women of lower classes, such as the

8. Accounts show that Charles provided handsomely for his illegitimate children and their families: for example, in 1672 and 1673, Monmouth received £43,000 from the king in gifts (his wife's earrings alone cost £1,200), the equivalent of nearly a quarter million pounds in today's currency. Maurice Lee, Jr., *The Heiresses of Buccleuch: Marriage, Money, and Politics in Seventeenth-Century Britain* (East Linton, Scotland: Tuckwell Press, 1996), 100–101.

actresses Mary "Moll" Davis and one of Charles's favorites, the comedian Nell Gwyn, but his later affair with the French Catholic aristocrat Louise Kéroualle, whom he made Duchess of Portsmouth and in 1680 gave a pension of £11,000 a year, caused riots in the streets of London.

James, too, had led an irregular life on the Continent, and he continued in his ways even after marrying one of his English mistresses and returning to England. His first marriage to Anne Hyde was a scandal, not so much because he had made her pregnant, but because a prince of the blood was marrying a commoner, the daughter of Edward Hyde, Charles's constant advisor during the Commonwealth and principal negotiator for the return of the Crown. Hyde would on the Restoration be named Charles's Lord Chancellor and receive the title Lord Clarendon. His daughter Anne, who was serving as a maid of honor in the court of James's sister Mary, the Princess of Orange, had begun the affair with James in 1659 while the court was still in exile in the Netherlands, and he had promised her marriage; however in 1660, when it became clear that the throne would be restored, and James was next in line in the succession, the match appeared worse than simply imprudent. When informed of James's intentions, his mother Queen Henrietta Maria was horrified, and Anne Hyde's own father urged that she be sent to the Tower for treason. Several of James's courtiers, including Anne Killigrew's distant relatives, Charles Berkeley and Henry Jermyn, attempted to invalidate the marriage by spreading rumors that Anne Hyde was so promiscuous that the child could be anyone's. Charles, having initially resisted the idea of the marriage, had, however, given his consent to it and refused to permit it to be annulled. Finally, in December 1660, James and Anne appeared in public as husband and wife, and Anne took over the running of their household, averaging £20,000 a year in expenses to support its size and opulence.[9]

James and Anne Hyde had two daughters who survived infancy, the princesses Mary and Ann; Mary would wed the Protestant Prince William of Orange and succeed her father to the throne in 1688, and Anne would become queen after her in 1702. Their mother Anne Hyde died in 1671; in 1673, James married a Catholic princess, Mary of Modena, and it became increasingly clear to Parliament and the

9. John Miller, "Anne, Duchess of York (1637–1671)," *ODNB*.

public that James himself was a practicing Catholic. This was the court in which Anne Killigrew would be listed as serving as one of the six maids of honor in 1683. Anne Killigrew's father, Henry Killigrew, thus found himself in the odd position of serving as an Anglican chaplain in an openly if not yet publicly acknowledged Catholic court. Matters came to a point of public crisis when there was a general anti-Catholic hysteria deliberately created by a group of conspirators attempting to ensure James would not succeed his brother. "The Popish Plot," which dominated the whole country's attention between 1678 and 1681, was largely the creation of Titus Oates, who along with several others alleged that a vast Catholic conspiracy was afoot in England to assassinate Charles; their fabricated evidence led to the highly publicized trials and executions of fifteen people before his perjury was finally revealed during the period when Anne Killigrew was a young adult.[10] This was contiguous with the highly factionalized Exclusion Crisis (1680–1683) when the Whig party in Parliament in opposition to the court or Tory party attempted to pass legislation that would make it impossible for a Catholic to succeed to the throne. The political and religious environment in which Anne Killigrew grew up was thus a highly contentious one involving the widespread use of propaganda and heated public debates, debates which because of the positions of her parents and relatives in the courts of Charles and James she could not avoid.

Restoration Court Culture and the Courtiers: Art and Literature

After years of poverty, the king and his court spent lavishly on restoring not only the presence of monarchy in England, but also in creating a spectacle of aristocratic power. Charles began recovering the royal art collection assembled by his father, which had been sold by Cromwell during the Commonwealth years; he also had to have new Crown jewels created for his coronation as their precious metals

10. For a detailed account of those involved in the plot, see John Kenyon, *The Popish Plot* (London: Heinemann, 1972) and for the issues relating to Catholicism and the succession, see John Miller, *Popery and Politics in England, 1660–1668* (Cambridge: Cambridge University Press, 1973), especially chapter 4.

had been melted down and their jewels sold.[11] The royal palace at Whitehall had been used for government offices and St. James's Palace for army barracks; many of the other royal valuables had been lost, sold, or hidden away. Thus the royal courts of Charles and his brother James not only had to be restored to power, but also to be recreated as the stages on which monarchy was presented.

Part of this recreation of monarchy included royal portraits, representations of the king, queen, and the members of their courts as the serene rulers of all they surveyed. Sir Peter Lely (1618–1680), who had painted the imprisoned Charles I with his children in the days before that king's execution, was the foremost portrait painter of his day in England; he had been maintained during the Commonwealth years by commissions from some of the most powerful aristocratic families in England.[12] In 1662, he was appointed the king's principal painter, thus succeeding to the post held before the war by Anthony Van Dyke. Although he painted Charles II several times and those paintings were widely circulated in copies, his primary patron was James, Duke of York, and members of his court. James's first wife, Anne Hyde, commissioned Lely in the early 1660s to paint a collection of portraits of the most beautiful women of her court and that of the queen, which came to be known as *The Windsor Beauties.*[13] He also received a commission from James to create a series of portraits of the naval officers who served under him in the naval battle of Lowestoft (1665). His most highly visible patron, however, was the king's mistress, Barbara Palmer, Countess of Castlemaine, who used the allegorical representations of herself in portraits as potent weapons in a war of reputations: she had Lely paint herself, accompanied by her children from the king, in the guise of the Virgin Mary, Athena goddess of wisdom, Mary Magdalene, and her namesake, St. Barbara, offering a direct and satiric challenge to the official portraits of Queen Catherine.[14]

11. Jerry Brotton, *The Sale of the Late King's Goods: Charles I and His Art Collection* (London: Pan Books, 2006).

12. Diana Dethloff, "Lely, Sir Peter (1618–1680)," *ODNB.*

13. See Lewis Melville, *The Windsor Beauties: Ladies of the Court of Charles II*, rev. ed. (Ann Arbor, MI: Victorian Heritage Press, 2005), "preface."

14. Julia Marciari Alexander, "Self-Fashioning and Portraits of Women at the Restoration Court: The Case of Peter Lely and Barbara Villiers, Countess of Castlemaine, 1660–1668"

Portraits, especially of members of court, thus functioned not only as artistic expressions but also as political statements.

There were two physical royal courts in London during Anne Killigrew's lifetime, that of Charles II and his queen at Whitehall and that of the Duke of York at St. James's Palace. The palace of Whitehall itself was not a royal residence in a traditional sense, being instead a conglomeration of buildings, consisting of some 1,500 rooms, resembling, as a French visitor in 1665 observed, "nothing but a heap of Houses, erected at divers times, and of different Models, which they made Contiguous in the best Manner they could for the Residence of the Court."[15] It was here that Anne Killigrew's mother, Judith, served as a lady in waiting to the queen, along with her cousin Elizabeth (married to Sir Francis Clinton) who served as the queen's dresser.[16] Her uncle, Sir William Killigrew, occupied rooms in Whitehall next to the royal family in his role as the queen's vice-chamberlain.

Her father Henry served the Duke of York at St. James's Palace, where he was appointed almoner to the duke and oversaw the chapel, as well as having an income from being a prebend of Westminster Abbey and serving as the master of the Savoy Hospital after 1663. The Savoy precinct like Whitehall was situated on the north shore of the Thames River; it included a former medieval palace that Henry VII had turned into a hospital for the poor in 1512. It was next to Somerset House, where the dowager queen Henrietta Maria resided before her return to France in 1665. Among the notable events at the Savoy marking the Restoration, was the Savoy Conference in 1661, when Charles II ordered an assembly of Anglican bishops and nonconformist ministers to meet in what ended up as an unsuccessful attempt to

---

(PhD diss., Yale University, 1999); Catharine MacLeod, "'Good but not Like': Peter Lely, Portrait Practice, and the Creation of a Court Look," in *Painted Ladies: Women at the Court of Charles II*, ed. Catharine MacLeod and Julia Marciari Alexander (London: National Portrait Gallery, 2001), 50–61.

15. Simon Thurley, *Whitehall Palace: An Architectural History of the Royal Apartments, 1240–1698* (New Haven, CT: Yale University Press, 1999), 99–126; Samuel de Sorbière, *A Voyage to England, Containing many Things relating to the State of Learning, Religion, and other Curiosities of that Kingdom* (London, 1709), 16–17.

16. J. P. Vander Motten, "Killigrew, Henry (1613–1700)," *ODNB*; J. P. Vander Motten, *Sir William Killigrew (1606–1695): His Life and Dramatic Works* (Ghent: Rijksuniversiteit te Gent, 1980), 30.

revise the Anglican liturgy to bring uniformity to Protestant worship in England. The Savoy precinct was also the home of the bookseller Samuel Lowndes, who would publish Henry's sermons as well as the posthumous edition of Anne's poems. It was in the chapel of the Savoy dedicated to St. John the Baptist that Killigrew's mother Judith was buried on February 2, 1683 and that Anne was buried on June 15, 1685.[17]

In addition to restoring the court at Whitehall, one of the first actions Charles took on returning to London was to reopen the theaters, which also played a significant part in the lives of the London Killigrews. He granted two royal patents to establish new theaters and acting companies, one to William Davenant whose company was called the Duke's Company, and one to Anne Killigrew's uncle, Thomas Killigrew, for the King's Company. Charles and the royalists who had been in exile had returned with a taste for French theater, which offered plays with heroic action and noble sentiments that made use of sophisticated scenery and staging, and most notably and unlike the English commercial theaters prior to the war, the French employed women as professional actors to play women's parts. Davenant had employed women as singers in his Commonwealth entertainments, but this would mark the first appearance of women on a London commercial stage as actresses rather than musicians or entertainers.[18]

The demand for new plays to be performed at the new theaters—the Theatre Royal housing the King's Company and the Dorset Garden Theatre for the Duke's Company—was met in part in the early 1660s by Charles's courtiers, including another of Anne Killigrew's uncles, Sir William Killigrew, and James Howard (c. 1640–1669) who married Anne Killigrew's cousin, the illegitimate Charlotte Jemina. William Killigrew's *Selindra* was the first newly written play performed by the King's Company on March 3, 1662.[19] It is a tragi-

17. *Register of the Chapel of St. John the Baptist, the Savoy*, London, Office of the Duchy of Lancaster, Royal Chapel of the Savoy Archive, February 2, 1683 and June 15, 1685.

18. For the earlier history of women as professional performers in England, see Clare McManus, "Women and English Renaissance Drama: Making and Unmaking 'The All-Male Stage,'" *Literature Compass* 4, no. 3 (2007): 784–96.

19. Nancy Klein Maguire, *Regicide and Restoration: English Tragicomedy, 1660–1671* (Cambridge: Cambridge University Press, 1992), 62.

comedy that blends a heroic plot centering on the restoration of the rightful queen of Hungary, who has been unjustly dispossessed of her throne, with a happily ending romance, clearly a pleasing topic for the new audience, and a subject which many of the new Restoration heroic dramas highlighted. In a commendatory verse prefacing the 1663 publication of the play, the unknown poet commends William Killigrew in terms that would be applied later to Anne: "thy wise, and modest Muse," it asserts, "breath'st a Noble Courtly Vein, / Such as may Caesar entertain."[20]

James Howard, the ninth son of Thomas Howard, 1st Earl of Berkshire, wrote two successful comedies that established the early pattern for what became known as the Restoration comedy of manners featuring the "witty couple." His *The English Monsieur* (1666) and *All Mistaken, or the Mad Couple* (1667), made the most of the acting talents of the leading male actor in Thomas Killigrew's company, Charles Hart, and a fresh young newcomer, Nell Gwyn. As was well known to those in their audiences, while they were portraying the dashing young man about town who won't be caught in the marriage trap and the clever beauty who wins his heart, Hart and Gwyn were in fact conducting a love affair offstage.[21] In 1667, she scored a tremendous success in John Dryden's *Secret Love, or The Maiden Queen*, and Samuel Pepys recorded in his diary for March 2, 1667 that the play, staged by Killigrew's company, entertained both Charles and James who were in the audience, and Nell's performance as Florimel was enchanting, "a mad[cap] girl, then most and best of all when she comes in like a young gallant; and hath the notions and carriage of a spark the most that ever I saw any man have."[22] Later in 1667, she would become Charles II's mistress and the subject of court paintings by Lely and others.

20. Sir William Killigrew, *Four New Plays viz: The seege of Urbin, Selindra, Love and frienship, Tragy-comedies, Pandora, a comedy* (Oxford, 1666), "The Latine Verses Translated," iv.

21. Elizabeth Howe, *The First English Actresses: Women and Drama, 1660–1700* (Cambridge: Cambridge University Press, 1992), 66; Felicity Nussbaum, "Actresses and the Economics of Celebrity, 1700–1800," in *Theatre and Celebrity in Britain, 1660–2000*, ed. Mary Luckhurst and Jane Moody (Basingstoke, UK: Palgrave Macmillan, 2005), 148–68.

22. Pepys, *Diary*, http://www.pepysdiary.com/archive/1667/03/02/.

The 1670s and early 1680s saw the full development of the dramas written for the new stages with their elaborate scenery and professional actresses. It is notable how many of them in the 1660s and 1670s were by writers associated with the court. Comedies by Charles's courtiers such as Sir Charles Sedley's *The Mulberry Garden*, William Wycherley's *The Country Wife*, and Sir George Etherege's *Man of Mode* all were set in contemporary London, with references to actual places and people. This style of comedy featured cynical young rake heroes, whose only occupation appears to be to live well and seduce beautiful young women. Dorimant, the hero of *Man of Mode*, was supposedly based on John Wilmot, Earl of Rochester, who was present in the audience watching as his character deftly manages multiple affairs: having fallen for the charms of the witty and wealthy Harriet, Dorimant nevertheless is willing to leave her company for an amorous rendezvous with the best friend of the mistress he has cast off at the start of the play. As one biographer has observed, "Restoration theatre has come to be seen as a guide to the values and attitudes of English society in the last decades of the seventeenth century, and not wholly without reason," noting additionally that between December 1666 and November 1667 Charles himself with his royal entourage attended twenty-two plays presented at court and by the King's Men in the Theatre Royal, in addition to visiting the rival company's productions.[23]

Both branches of the royal family were patrons of the arts, especially the theaters, and it is clear that both the male and female courtiers were actively engaged in establishing the culture of the courts through their writings and performances. John Wilmot, Earl of Rochester, and John Sheffield, 1st Duke of Buckingham and Normanby, for example, were particularly well known for their abilities to create amusing impromptu verses, and both were patrons of John Dryden and other professional writers. Both men also penned serious satires and were deeply engaged with literary matters, with Sheffield's *An Essay on Poetry*, modeled after Horace's *Ars Poetica*, going through multiple editions after it was printed in 1682. John Dryden, the poet laureate, created a steady stream of dramas first for Killigrew's com-

23. Derek Wilson, *All the King's Women: Love, Sex, and Politics in the Life of Charles II* (London: Hutchinson, 2003), 225, 229.

pany and then for Davenant's in the 1670s, but he was also during this time beginning to publish important translations of classical writers including Ovid and the historian Plutarch, making available to readers who had not received classical education or university training the rich classical tradition which so marks Killigrew's verse. In the late 1670s, he published scathing satires on the leading figures in the Popish Plot and the political parties, culminating in 1681 with the publication of *Absalom and Achitophel*, but he also produced the following year in 1682 *Religio laici*, or "the layman's faith," a long poem calling for reason and moderation in religious beliefs to avoid the conflicts of extreme sects both Protestant and Catholic.

In 1675 when Anne Killigrew was fifteen, the court mounted an elaborate and expensive masque, *Calisto, or the chaste nymph* by John Crowne, which highlighted the acting talents of the young princesses and the ladies of the court. The jewels on the costumes were astonishing, being estimated by one attendee, John Evelyn, as being nearly £20,000 worth on the costume of goddess Diana, played by the maid of honor Margaret Blagge; the account records show that her costume was made from twenty-four yards of gold brocade and one hundred and forty-six yards of gold and silver lace in addition to a quiver with sixteen arrows.[24] As with the earlier masques of Charles I's court, the play is a celebration of the royal family and the prosperity of the country under their reign: the character of the River Thames declares, "Pleasure, Arts, Religion, Glory, / Warm'd by his propitious Smile, / Flourish there, and bless this Isle."[25] The stage direction states that the "Genius of England" then gestures toward the royal family in the audience, exclaiming, "But stay! What wonder does my spirit seize? / See! Here are both the great Divinities," and the Thames confirms, "The God and Goddess too of this bless'd Isle!" thus turning the whole court audience into part of an ideal pastoral world, one filled with youth, beauty, peace, and prosperity. The irony, surely not lost on many, was that the woman portraying the Thames was none other than Charles's former mistress, Mary "Moll" Davis.

24. John Evelyn, *The Life of Margaret Godolphin* (London: Chatto and Windus, 1907), 67; Eleanore Boswell, *The Restoration Court Stage (1660–1702)* (New York: Barnes and Noble, 1932), 323–24.

25. John Crowne, *Calisto, or the chaste nymph* (London, 1675), "Prologue," sig.b2r.

Thus while the world of the court was glamorous, luxurious, cultured, and literate, it was simultaneously laced with irony and the grim struggles of self-seeking men and women to hold on to their tenuous positions there. The women associated with the court were sometimes as notorious in their public behaviors as the men. Charles's and James's young mistresses, many of whom served as maids of honor, frequently scandalized Samuel Pepys, who recorded an example on February 8, 1663:

> Captain. Ferrers telling me, among other Court passages, how about a month ago, at a ball at Court, a child was dropped [miscarried] by one of the ladies in dancing, but nobody knew who, it being taken up by somebody in their handkerchief. The next morning all the Ladies of Honor appeared early at Court for their vindication, so that nobody could tell whose this mischance should be. But it seems Mrs. Wells fell sick that afternoon, and hath disappeared ever since, so that it is concluded that it was her.[26]

A French visitor to the court, the Count Grammont, likewise noted that "Lady Middleton, Lady Denham, the queen's and the duchess's maids of honor, and a hundred others, bestow their favors to the right and to the left, and not the least notice is taken of their conduct. As for Lady Shrewsbury, she is conspicuous. I would take a wager she might have a man killed for her every day, find she would only hold her head the higher for it."[27]

Charles II appears to have been cynically amused by the real-life exploits of the young people in his court as well as entertained by the fictional ones on stage in Thomas Killigrew's theater.[28] Bishop Gilbert Burnet, writing about Charles in hindsight, declared that after

26. Pepys, *Diary*, http://www. pepysdiary. com/archive/1667/03/02/.

27. Anthony Hamilton, *The Memoirs of Count Grammont*, ed. Gordon Goodwin, 2 vols. (Edinburgh: John Grant, 1908), 2:3.

28. For an account of Charles's relationships with his courtiers, see Jeremy Webster, *Performing Libertinism in Charles II's Court: Politics, Drama, Sexuality* (London: Palgrave Macmillan, 2005), Chapter 1.

returning from exile, Charles had "a very ill opinion both of men and women; and did not think there was either sincerity or chastity in the world out of principle, but that some had either the one or the other out of humor or vanity. He thought that nobody served him out of love: and so he was quits with the entire world, and loved others as little as he thought they loved him."[29] Sexual intrigues were very often associated with political stakes, especially by contemporary satirists. Rochester wrote in 1673 after the marriage of James and Mary of Modena a nasty little lyric, "Signior Dildo," sardonically welcoming the Italian sex toy to England and describing the enthusiastic welcome he would be given by the various maids of honor and women of the court, whom he caricatures by name: writing of the widowed Mary, Countess of Falmouth, who had been married to a distant relative of Anne Killigrew's, Rochester snipes, "The Countess of Falmouth, of whom people tell / Her footmen wear shirts of guinea an ell, / Might save the expense if she did but know / How lusty a young swinger is Signior Dildo."[30] George Villiers, Duke of Buckingham, contributed in 1678 his "Character of an Ugly Woman," attacking the "mother" of the maids of honor in Mary of Modena's court: as one commentator noted, of all the male court wits, only Sir Charles Sedley did not have any antifemale satires credited to him.[31] In 1681, the anonymous author of the mocking satire "An Heroic Poem" (included in Appendix 4 in this volume) likewise targets the sexual and political activities of individual court women, as well as the hypocrisy and greed of the men, in his attack on Whig politicians and supporters of Monmouth's claim to the throne, in the courts of which Anne Killigrew and her family served.

The women at court, however, whose virtue was above question in such satires were the royal wives, Queen Catherine and Princess Mary of Modena, and, of course, there were numerous women who served them who are simply less known to later generations precisely because they did not embrace a libertine lifestyle and thus become

29. Gilbert Burnet, *History of my own Time*, ed. O. Airy, 2 vols (Oxford, 1897–1900), 1:168.

30. *The Works of John Wilmot, Earl of Rochester*, ed. Harold Love (Oxford: Oxford University Press, 1999), 248–57.

31. John Harold Wilson, *The Court Wits of the Restoration* (Princeton: Princeton University Press, 1948), 123–25.

fodder for gossip and satire. Unlike the glamorous courtesan beauties painted by Lely and celebrated by Count Grammont, many women serving in these courts were, like Anne Killigrew's mother, married to others also in royal service. There were various ranks of those who served in female royal households, most having been established during Queen Elizabeth I's long reign, all of whom received salaries, and their titles indicate their relative importance through the degree of access they had to the royal person.

The most important of the ladies in waiting was the Mistress of the Robes, followed by the ladies of the bedchamber, and by the women of the bedchamber, who during this time came to be referred to as dressers. The ladies of the bedchamber were peeresses of the realm and were frequently the wives or daughters of leading political figures or members of the king's councils. These women escorted their royal mistress in her public appearances and assisted her in the formal ceremonial tasks of dressing and dining. The women of the bedchamber, such as Anne Killigrew's aunt, Anne Killigrew Kirke, who served Queen Henrietta Maria as a dresser, Anne's mother Judith, and her cousin Elizabeth Clinton, were ladies in waiting serving Queen Catherine. These were gentlewomen who assisted their royal mistress in more mundane daily tasks such as doing her hair, keeping her clothes, waiting on her at the table, accompanying her on walks, and nursing her when she was ill. These women served on a weekly rotation, during which time they were at their mistresses' beck and call both day and night and would sleep in the royal bedchamber. The widow Lady Tuke, writing in 1682 to her friend Mary Evelyn, John Evelyn's wife, about her position as a lady in waiting, lamented that "there is nothing has troubled me more since I had the honor to serve the Queen than that restraint of my liberty… . it makes life less pleasing to me, and really makes one value the world very little, nor that grinning honor which many esteem."[32]

Salaries for such positions could be lucrative, but the courts of Charles and James came under financial constraints in the 1660s. In 1663, it was announced that royal servants would no longer be fed at royal expense, but would instead be paid wages to cover their board,

32. Frances Harris, *Transformations of Love: The Friendship of John Evelyn and Margaret Godolphin* (London: Oxford University Press, 2002), 105.

ranging from £547 for the Mistress of the Robes to £60 for a dresser, with additional stipends given based on seniority between £150 and £200 a year.[33] The exceptions to this were the maids of honor, whose meals according to records cost the crown £700 a year, with a £200 yearly pension. The maids of honor, like the pages of the male royals, were the youngest members of the royal courts; Anne Killigrew's uncle, Sir William Killigrew, had entered into the service of the princes of Orange when he was thirteen. They did not serve in the bedchamber itself, but participated in public court functions, interacting with visitors, performing in court entertainments, and forming a decorative entourage for their mistress or master at public events. The maids of honor shared a room with one other, had a "closet" or small private room for writing and devotion, and a common room to receive visitors.[34] Commentators are in general agreement that the families of these maids of honor sent their daughters to court primarily to secure good husbands, that is, well-to-do and titled ones, and their appointment was very often a reward for services to the court by their families. Spectacular marriages could be made this way: as has been pointed out, Anne Hyde, Duchess of York, was a maid of honor, as was Margaret, Duchess of Newcastle, and Frances Stuart, "La Belle Stuart," fended off the king's advances to become Duchess of Lennox and Richmond.[35] As glamorous as this life may seem, it was easy for these young women to fall into debt; they had to provide their own clothes suitable for royal events, and those serving the queen received a stipend of only £10, while those serving the duchess received only £20, and the popular recreation of card playing and gambling also could be a young person's downfall.

A maid of honor who was noted for her piety and distaste of the libertine lifestyles that surrounded her, Margaret Blagge (1652–1678), also had numerous points of connection with people in Anne Killigrew's life. In 1666 she became a maid of honor to Anne Hyde, Duchess of York, and in 1671 on her death, Margaret Blagge became a maid of honor in the court of Queen Catherine. In 1672, she met through

33. Anne Somerset, *Ladies in Waiting from the Tudors to the Present Day* (London: Weidenfeld and Nicolson, 1984), 134.

34. Harris, *Transformations*, 107.

35. Harris, *Transformations*, 106–7.

his wife Mary the author and diarist John Evelyn, who became her spiritual counselor and close friend. John Evelyn's preservation of his correspondence with Margaret Blagge and his celebratory biography written after her death, *The Life of Margaret Godolphin* (first printed in 1847 as *The Life of Mrs. Godolphin*), a memorial to her piety and goodness, gives us an alternative picture of court life as experienced by a devout Christian single woman.

Having nursed Anne Hyde through her final illness, the young Margaret Blagge reflected on the fate of those who once were celebrated for their position and influence. "The D[uch]ess died, a Prince honored, in power: had much Wit, much more esteem," wrote the young Margaret, "None remembered her after one Week: None sorry for her. She smelt extremely; was tossed and flung about, & everyone did what they would with that stately Carcass."[36] "What is this World!" she exclaimed, "What is Greatness! What to be esteem'd & thought a Wit! We shall all be stripped, without Sense or Remembrance: But God, if we serve him in our Health, will give us Patience in our Sickness."

Although she was an extremely attractive young woman and had several suitors, the one who eventually won her heart was a rising young courtier, Sidney Godolphin, who had entered Charles II's court as a page in 1662 and had risen to the post of groom of the bedchamber, an important position that offered personal contact with the king and involved attending the king in his private rooms and assisting at meals.[37] Even so, the couple lacked sufficient funds to marry until 1675, and Margaret herself was constantly torn between marriage and the desire to lead a single life devoted to God. While in the court, her diaries show that she divided her time between serving her royal mistress and retiring into her room for private devotion and study, leaving behind a group of manuscripts containing her meditations and prayers which Evelyn preserved.

Evelyn, who had initially welcomed the return of Charles II, soon became disgusted and dismayed by the libertine atmosphere,

36. Evelyn, *Life of Margaret Godolphin*, 9.

37. R. O. Bucholz, "The Bedchamber: Grooms of the Bedchamber, 1660–1837," in *Court Officers, 1660–1837* (London: Institute for Historical research, 2006), 20–24, at *British History Online*, http://www.british-history.ac.uk/report.aspx?compid=43768.

and he found in Margaret Blagge his exemplar for feminine piety. As Blagge's cousin, John North noted, even in the court one could find among the women "as many truly pious and strictly religious as could be found in any other resort whatsoever."[38] In 1673, after seven years of service, Margaret was determined to leave the world of the court and devote herself to religion, and she turned to a distant relative of Anne Killigrew's to assist her. Lady Berkeley had been formerly the groom of the stole in Anne Hyde, Duchess of York's service (a position of some responsibility involving keeping of the robes of state and dressing the duchess on state occasions), and she had subsequently joined the queen's household. Christiana, Lady Berkeley (1639–1698), was the daughter of a wealthy East India merchant and president of the Levant trading company Sir Andrew Riccard; she had been married and widowed twice before marrying Sir John Berkeley, 1st Baron Berkeley of Stratton. Berkeley was the son of Elizabeth Killigrew, a distant relative of Anne's branch of the family, and as a boy he had grown up with her father and uncles. It is to this Lady Berkeley that Anne Killigrew addresses one of her occasional poems, and two of Anne Killigrew's paintings now are preserved at Berkeley Castle.[39]

When Margaret Blagge decided to leave court life, she turned to Lady Berkeley to provide a place for her to live. On being granted the queen's permission to resign her post, Evelyn records, she returned to her room and fell upon her knees: "she Bless'd God, as for a Signal Deliverance: She was come out of Egypt, & now on her Way to the Land of Promise."[40] Margaret Blagge was thought to have left the court in order to be married to Godolphin, but in fact she had decided against marriage, yearning for a life of celibate devotion not dissimilar to Anne Killigrew's frequent rejection of secular love over spiritual in her poems. Margaret did eventually marry her patient suitor in 1675, but died when giving birth in 1678.

Almost a decade after her death, in his diary entry for February 6, 1685, John Evelyn recorded his dismay over what the Restoration had become:

38. Harris, *Transformations*, 134.

39. One is a full-length self-portrait, and one is of an unknown lady.

40. Evelyn, *Life of Margaret Godolphin*, 32–33.

> I am never to forget the inexpressible luxury, & prophaness, gaming, & all dissolution, and as it were total forgetfulness of God (it being Sunday Evening) which this day sennight, I was witness of; the King, sitting & toying with his Concubines Portsmouth, Cleveland, & Mazarine &c: A French boy singing love songs, in that glorious Gallery, whilst about 20 of the great Courtiers & other dissolute persons were at Basset [a high-stakes card game] round a large Table, a bank of at least 2000 in Gold before them ... and surely as they thought would never have an End: six days after was all in the dust.[41]

On February 2, Charles II suddenly fell ill and by February 6 was dead. His brother James was now crowned James II and his wife became Queen Mary. There is presently no known record of Anne Killigrew's participation in any of these events. The last record we have of her concerns her own death from small pox only a few months later in June, 1685, thus making both her birth and her death coincide with the reign of Charles II.

Anne Killigrew: Life

As we have seen, Anne Killigrew was born into a family of courtiers. The Killigrew family was originally from Cornwall, with one branch settling in London. Through her grandmother, Mary Woodhouse (1590–1650), Anne Killigrew was connected to the learned daughters of Sir Anthony Cooke, who, like Queen Elizabeth I, had been educated like young men along humanist principles. Through the marriage of the sister of her grandfather, Sir Robert Killigrew (1579–1633), Anne Killigrew was a cousin to the powerful family of the Berkeleys of Stratton. Anne Killigrew's father, uncles, and aunts were born either at Hanworth, near Hampton Court, or in London, and they all, in various ways, served the royal family. As a biographer of her uncle, Thomas Killigrew, commented about that generation, "in many ways

41. John Evelyn, *The Diary of John Evelyn*, ed. E. S. De Beer, 6 vols. (Oxford: Clarendon Press, 1955), 4:413–14.

this family illustrates the curious social usages of the time. A daughter of Robert Killigrew became mistress to the King while a son preached eloquent sermons to him at Whitehall; another son fought his battles in England while a third, as we shall see, borrowed money for him and amused him while he danced away his time in exile."[42]

When one looks at Anne Killigrew's female relatives, it is striking how many of them served royal mistresses. Her aunt, Anne Killigrew Kirke (1607–1641), was a much loved member of the court of Queen Henrietta Maria, serving as her dresser, a position which gave her considerable access to the queen. Charles I himself attended the wedding when she married George Kirke in January 1627; he eventually became groom of the bedchamber to Charles I. In 1633, this Anne had acted with Queen Henrietta Maria in the court performance of Walter Montagu's *Shepherd's Paradise*; in the 1659 publication of the play, she is listed as playing the part of the shepherdess Camena.[43] When she died in an accident on the Thames, poets lamented her loss and the queen grieved; a generation later, Anne Killigrew would use her aunt's tragic fate in her poetry as foreshadowing the war and its losses. Another aunt, Katherine, served as a maid of honor to the Princess Royal of Orange at the request of the then Prince Charles, who wrote on her behalf to his aunt, the Queen of Bohemia; on Katherine's death, her place as a maid of honor was taken by Anne Hyde, who there caught the eye of the future Duke of York.[44]

Perhaps the most notorious of her aunts, however, was the previously mentioned Elizabeth (1622–1681), who married on October 24, 1639 Francis Boyle, the son of the Earl of Cork, who was the brother of the scientist Robert Boyle and the dramatist Roger Boyle, the future Earl of Orrey. This made her the sister-in-law of the pious Mary Boyle, the future Countess of Warwick. She recorded in her autobiography how the two young girls had been very close during this period: "My brother being then judged too young to live with his wife," Mary Boyle wrote, he "was a day or two after celebrating the marriage

42. Alfred Harbage, *Thomas Killigrew: Cavalier Dramatist, 1612–83* (Philadelphia: University of Pennsylvania Press, 1930), 38.

43. Motten, *Sir William Killigrew*, 12–13; *Calendar of State Papers, Domestic Series, of the Reign of Charles I, 1641–1643*, ed. William Douglas Hamilton (London, 1887), 53.

44. Harbage, *Thomas Killigrew*, 28.

(which was done before the King and Queen) at Whitehall (she being then a maid of honor to the Queen) sent into France to travel, and his wife then brought home to our house, where she and I became chamber-fellows."[45] She notes that while she very much enjoyed the company of the spritely young Elizabeth Killigrew, in hindsight she blames her for having a "great and ruling power with me; and by her having so brought me to be very vain and foolish, enticing me to spend (as she did) her time in seeing and reading plays and romances, and in exquisite and curious dressing."[46] The blame, one feels, cannot entirely fall on Elizabeth, however, as Mary Boyle had in 1638 defied her parents who had arranged a very advantageous match for her. Instead, she later fell in love with Charles Rich (1616–1673), the second son of the Earl of Warwick, whom she apparently met through Elizabeth; Elizabeth "had many of the young gallants that she was acquainted with at Court that came to visit her at the Savoy (where we lived)," among whom was Charles Rich, although at that time "he was then in love with a maid of honour to the Queen, one Mrs. Hareson [Harrison], that had been chamber-fellow to my sister-in-law whilst she lived at Court."[47] The house in the Savoy in which the strong-willed Mary shared her room with Elizabeth was the same house that Henry Killigrew and his family would occupy nearly thirty years later.[48]

Anne Killigrew was the third of five children born to Henry and Judith. Henry (1613–1700) was educated at Christ Church, Oxford. While a student there, he contributed verses to several student collections, including some in Latin in *Britanniae natalis* (1630) to celebrate the birth of the child who would become Charles II. Notably, he also wrote an entertainment to be performed at the wedding of Charles Herbert, the son of the Earl of Pembroke, and Mary Villiers, the daughter of the Duke of Buckingham. The play, perhaps oddly for a wedding, was a tragedy, *The Conspiracy*, but it was not performed, although it was poorly published in 1638 and reprinted in a corrected

45. Mary Rich, *The Autobiography of Mary Countess of Warwick*, ed. T. Crofton Croker (London, 1848), 4.

46. Rich, *Autobiography*, 4.

47. Rich, *Autobiography*, 5.

48. Flora Masson, *Robert Boyle: A Biography* (London: Constable, 1914), 83–84.

version in 1653 entitled *Pallantus and Eudora*.[49] In 1638, as the troubles between Charles I and Parliament were mounting, young Henry, now an MA of Oxford, was traveling in Italy; at some point in the late 1630s, he became a minister. When the war began, he was back in England, and served as a chaplain in the king's army, and in 1642, he was appointed a chaplain to James, Duke of York.[50] He, like many of his family members including his sisters and their families, would accompany the defeated royal family into exile on the Continent.

It is not yet known when he married Judith, or who her family was. What we do know of her comes from traces of her in her later life as a lady in waiting and as a member of the court's group of talented musicians. She is several times mentioned in the letters of a European visitor, the Dutch poet and composer Constantijn Huygens (1596–1687), and two of his short letters to her have been preserved. Sir Robert Killigrew, Anne's grandfather, had entertained Huygens on his stay in England as a diplomat in the 1620s; scholars believe that it was Robert Killigrew who gave a manuscript copy of John Donne's verses to Huygens, Donne having served as a chaplain on a diplomatic mission with Sir Robert.[51] Thus Huygens appears to have enjoyed a long-standing literary and musical association with the extended Killigrew family into which Judith married. Huygens was a secretary to the princes of Orange, including the future King William III and could well have known many in the English exile community who settled in The Hague, such as Judith's brother-in-law, Thomas Killigrew, who married a Dutch woman there in 1655.[52] Judith appears in Huygen's letters in the early 1670s. In one letter, he recommends her to French acquaintances visiting England as an ingenious lady and an

49. In the 1722 edition of collected works of the courtier poet and dramatist Sir Charles Sedley (bap. 1639–1701), a shortened version of this play was published under the title "The Tyrant King of Crete." Sedley's biographer suggested Killigrew gave the piece to Sedley to adapt; Sedley's daughter Catherine (1657–1717) was a maid of honor in the queen's court after 1678 and had been James's long-time mistress while Anne Killigrew was at court. See V. de Sola Pinto, *Sir Charles Sedley, 1639–1701: A Study in the Life and Literature of the Restoration* (London: Constable and Company, 1927), 280–81.

50. Motten, "Killigrew, Henry (1613–1700)," *ODNB*.

51. Motten, *Sir William Killigrew*, 23.

52. J. P. Vander Motten, "Thomas Killigrew's 'Lost Years,' 1655–1660," *Neophilologus* 82, no. 2 (1998): 317.

accomplished musician, and in two others written to her, he playfully inquires after her health, hoping her lute is still in tune, and sending her some of his short compositions.[53]

The other trace we presently have of Judith Killigrew is a signed copy of a second folio edition of *Mr. William Shakespeares Comedies, Histories, and Tragedies* (1632).[54] The signature, "Judith Killigrew," appears on the title page; while the Folger Shakespeare Library does not have a record of the volume's provenance prior to its purchase in 1916, the curatorial notes on the volume state, "The Judith Killigrew who wrote her name on the title may be presumed to have owned the volume in which the title originally stood. That she was the Judith who was wife to Henry Killigrew, D.D. (1613–1700), divine and master of the Savoy, and herself died in 1683 need not be doubted. The handwriting of the signature fits well enough with the date of her death." From these slender clues, we now can begin to fill in the family in which Anne Killigrew was born and raised, a family who valued music and literature and who had been servants of the court throughout their lives, both in exile and in the restored courts.

After the death of Judith in 1683, Henry appears to have turned more toward publishing his devotional writing and other literary pursuits. He had separately printed several of his sermons preached before the king, and in 1685 he collected them in *Sermons Preached Partly before His Majesty at White-Hall and Partly before Anne Dutchess of York, at the Chappel at St. James* (1685); the letter from the publisher to the reader is dated January 26, 1685, suggesting that it was published before Anne's death. The publisher explains that they were aware that "there are so many Sermons, upon all sorts of Subjects, already extant; that the Author of these, had he been perfectly left to his own liberty, would not have increased the Number"; however, he was prevailed to do so by "some near Relations, that is, were desirous to converse with him, by the help of these Discourses, when he is dead"—in short, fam-

53. Constantijn Huygens, *De briefwisseling van Constantijn Huygens, 1608–1687*, ed. E. C. M. Huysman, letters 287, 310, 314, and 6862, at *Historici.nl: Vindplaats voor de geschiedenis van Nederland*, http://www.historici.nl/Onderzoek/Projecten/Huygens.

54. Folger Shakespeare Library, shelfmark STC 22274 Fo. 2 no 31.

ily members desiring to have his voice and counsel preserved.[55] The publisher describes Henry Killigrew's sermons as combining rhetorical skill with a wholesome content: "they both instruct and delight; satisfie the appetite, and excite it; present solid nourishment, and give it a grateful taste."

In the 1680s and 1690s, Henry was writing verse and also engaged with translating: *Select Epigrams of Martial, translated into English* (1689); *Innocui Sales. A Collection of New Epigrams with a Praefatory Essay on Epigrammatic Poetry* (1694); *Epigrams of Martial, Englished. With some Other Pieces, Ancient and Modern* (1695); *A Book of New Epigrams. By the Same Hand that Translated Martial* (1695); and *A Court of Judicature, in Imitation of Libanius. With New Epigrams. By the Hand that translated Martial* (1697). Henry Killigrew's preference for the short, witty epigram is significant given his daughter's choice of poetic forms. She has several in her surviving work, and these were the poems for which we have manuscript copies suggesting circulation, even though Henry Killigrew declares that the best epigrams reveal a "Masculine Acuteness in particular which an Epigram requires."[56] In his essay on epigrams, he states that "an Epigram gives as strong and ample a proof of any Man's Abilities in Poetry, as the longest and most elaborate piece can do. A Man's *Wit, Judgment*, and *Literature*, may be seen plainly in a *few Lines* … and that he writes no more, must be imputed to his want of Leisure, Industry or Ambition."[57] The epigram, designed to be a short, witty comment on a person or type, lends itself to a sophisticated social critique, a moral presented in a clever and skillful package.

By 1693, Henry had opened his rooms in Westminster Abbey to his aging older brother, Sir William.[58] William had resigned his position as vice-chancellor to the queen in 1682. Like his brother, he, too, turned to publishing his devotional writings and literary thoughts. The title of the first edition displays the courtier's combination of ironic wit and personal melancholy in the context of the issues of the

55. Henry Killigrew, *Sermons, Preached Partly before His Majesty at White-Hall* (London, 1685), sig. A2r–v.

56. Henry Killigrew, *Innocui Sales. A Collection of New Epigrams* (London, 1694), sig. A7v.

57. Killigrew, *Innocui*, sig. A5r.

58. Motten, *Sir William Killigrew*, 148.

day: *Mid-night Thoughts, Writ, as some think, by a London-Whigg, or, a Westminster-Tory; Others think by a Quaker, or, a Jesuit: But call him what they please, they may find him a true Penitent of the Church of Christ* (1682). The subtitle also is revealing: *The Constant Meditations of a Man who for many years built on Sand, which every blast of cross Fortune has defaced. But now he has laid new Foundations on the Rock of his Salvation, which no Storms can shake; and will out-last the Conflagration of the World, when time shall melt into Eternity*. It was reprinted several times before William's death in 1695, each time augmented with commendatory poems and letters from friends and admirers of the book.

Some of Anne's numerous cousins may have been a part of her life at court, albeit in the case of the most notorious, not a very reputable one. Her cousin Henry (1637–1705?), typically referred to as Harry, was the son of Thomas Killigrew by his first marriage to the maid of honor Cecelia Crofts: Thomas's biographer writes of him coldly that "Harry became a courtier and a scoundrel… . it is largely owing to his actions that his father's name has been one of such ill repute down to our own day." "It would be difficult to point to a worse rogue than Henry Killigrew among all the rakes and scoundrels who afflicted the Restoration court," he concludes.[59] Having been raised in England, the young Harry joined the Duke of York's entourage in the late 1650s and served in various capacities, including being one of the courtiers who swore that he had been intimate with Anne Hyde in an attempt to have James's marriage to her annulled. "He was of a sprightly and witty humor," the Count Grammont declares, and "had the art of telling a story in the most entertaining manner, by the graceful and natural turn he could give it."[60] In fact, his nickname at court was "Lying Killigrew," and he was a member of the notorious group of young rakes, "the Ballers," a group led by Wilmot, the Earl of Rochester, devoted to "drinking, sexual exhibitions, and dancing naked with the young women in a brothel kept by 'Lady' Bennett."[61] Samuel Pepys

59. Harbage, *Thomas Killigrew*, 108, 120.

60. Hamilton, *Memoirs of Count Grammont*, 2:25.

61. John H. Wilson, *A Rake and His Times: George Villiers, 2nd Duke of Buckingham* (New York: Farrar, Straus and Young, 1954), 37; James William Johnson, *A Profane Wit: The Life of John Wilmot, Earl of Rochester* (Rochester, NY: University of Rochester Press, 2004), 106.

recorded in his diary several chance encounters with Harry Killigrew, none of them pleasant: on September 1, 1666, he along with his wife attended the playhouse, "but were there horribly frighted to see Young Killigrew come in with a great many more young sparks; but we hid ourselves, so as we think they did not see us. By and by, they went away, and then we were at rest again." Harry at this time held the important post of groom of the bedchamber for James's court, the same in which Anne's father served as almoner and chaplain. On May 30, 1668, Pepys encountered him again, this time having returned from a brief exile in France, and Pepys found himself both fascinated and horrified: "Harry Killigrew, a rogue newly come back out of France, but still in disgrace at our Court, and young Newport and others, as very rogues as any in the town, who were ready to take hold of every woman that come by them," Pepys noted. "But, Lord! their mad bawdy talk did make my heart ache! And here I first understood by their talk the meaning of the company that lately were called Ballets [Ballers]... dancing naked, and all the roguish things in the world."[62]

What we do know of Anne's own birth and early days comes from notes by her father and uncle given to the antiquarian writer Anthony à Wood, who had written to them asking for family information for his biographical history of alumni of Oxford University.[63] According to this source, Anne was born in London and "christened in a private chamber, when the offices in the common-prayer were not publicly allowed," that is to say, early in 1660 before the restoration of the Church of England. We presently know little about her upbringing and education other than that she was "tenderly educated" and "became most admirable in the arts of poetry and painting."[64] At this point in time, we have no further details about her formal education, such as whether or not she could read in Latin the classics which so infuse her own verse; as we have seen, her father was a skilled Latinist and interested in translation, but whether Anne Killigrew followed in his footsteps, or made use of the numerous editions of English translations of the classics appearing during this period, we do not know.

62. Pepys, *Diary*, http://www.pepysdiary.com.

63. Motten, *Sir William Killigrew*, 132.

64. Anthony à Wood, *Athenae Oxonienses*, rev. ed., ed. P. Bliss, 4 vols. (1813–20), 4:621.

Likewise, it is unclear where she might have received her training as an artist. It is not insignificant that her portrait of James as the Duke of York held in the Royal Collection was attributed to Sir Peter Lely, the court portrait painter, until a modern cleaning revealed her signature.[65] A fixture at court, Lely surely would have been known to various members of the Killigrew family, and he had painted a portrait of her uncle Thomas's second wife, Charlotte Hess. Lely had occupied the same house in Covent Garden from 1650 until his death in 1680, and his studio was visited by all the court beauties as well as those interested in art. Anne Killigrew's treatment of the darkened pastoral landscapes in her portraits are highly reminiscent of his backdrops for portraits, specifically those of Jane Needham, Mrs. Middleton (c. 1663–65), Elizabeth Wriothesley, Countess of Northumberland (1665), and the early portrait of Anne Hyde as Duchess of York (1660).

One of the visitors to Lely's studio who might also have had some acquaintance with the Killigrew family was the successful commercial portrait painter Mary Beale (1633–1699). She had set up her own London studio in Pall Mall in 1670 and greatly benefited from Lely's friendship.[66] Assisted by her family—her husband organized not only the commissions and payments but also mixed her paints, and her sons assisted in the completion of the portraits—Mary Beale was able to train and employ women as her assistants as well. The Beale's London house in the 1670s and 1680s was a meeting place for rising men in the Royal Society of London as well as the church, including the future archbishops of Canterbury, John Tillotson and Thomas Tenison, both of whom were known to Henry Killigrew.[67] Mary Beale was also was a writer, leaving behind an essay on the divine nature of friendship addressed to Tillotson's wife Elizabeth, a treatment of the topic which would have resonated with the young Anne Killigrew.[68]

65. L. Cust and C. H. C. Baker, "Notes," *Burlington Magazine* 28, no. 153 (1916): 112–13, 116.

66. Christopher Reeve, "Beale, Mary (bap. 1633, d. 1699)," *ODNB*.

67. Elizabeth Walsh and Richard Jeffree, *The Excellent Mrs. Mary Beale* (London: Inner London Education Authority, 1975), 12.

68. Mary Beale, London, British Library, MS Harley 6828, fols. 510r–23v; Tabitha Barber, *Mary Beale: Portrait of a Seventeenth-Century Painter, Her Family, and Her Studio* (London: Geffrye Museum Trust, 1999), 8.

While there is presently no evidence indicating that Anne Killigrew studied with either of these artists, it is clear that during the period she was growing up, she would have had the opportunity to observe their work.

Anne was the youngest of three sisters. Her sisters, Mary (born prior to 1650) and Elizabeth (c. 1650–1701), may have been born or raised on the Continent in their early years, given that their father was in the service of the Duke of York, and it was not uncommon for wives with children to follow their husbands into exile. Anne Killigrew's sisters have received little attention, in part perhaps because unlike their other female relatives, they both married and resided outside court circles. Mary wed Nicholas Only, a clerk at Wheathampstead, on August 14, 1665, and Elizabeth married the Reverend John Lambe (1650–1708) on May 8, 1673.[69] In 1663, Henry Killigrew had been granted the living at Wheathampstead in Hertfordshire as one of his incomes. John Lambe is listed on the marriage application as being the rector of Wheathampstead, and in 1673, Henry Killigrew resigned from that position, apparently in favor of his new-son-in-law.

It would appear from his daughters' marriages to men associated with the church in Wheathampstead that the Killigrews may have at some time resided in this ancient village, whose origins go back the Romans, with its famous "Devil's Dyke," an ancient fortification ditch. The church, St. Helens, was begun in the thirteenth century and completed in the fourteenth century; the valuable farming lands about it were given in 1060 by King Edward the Confessor to Westminster Abbey, of which Henry Killigrew was a prebend and where he would live during his final years.[70] Of Mary and her family, nothing more is presently known, but Elizabeth bore five sons and five daughters before passing away in Wheathampstead on October 28, 1701. For two

69. Hertfordshire County Council, "Marriages and Marriage Licenses (1538–1922)," *Hertfordshire Names Online* (HNO), https://www.hertsdirect.org/ufs/. I am indebted to Suzanne Nicholls at the Hertfordshire Archives and Local Studies Centre for confirming this information.

70. Derek Vincent Stern, *A Hertfordshire Demesne of Westminster Abbey: Profits, Productivity, and Weather* (Hatfield: University of Hertfordshire Press, 2001), 48, 51; William Page, "Wheathampstead with Harpenden: Churches and Charities," in *The Victoria History of the County of Hertford*, vol. 2 (London: A. Constable, 1908), 309–14, at *British History Online*, http://www.british-history.ac.uk/report.aspx?compid=43283&strquery=wheathampstead.

of the Killigrew daughters, it appears, their lives were lived far from the courts and the riotous behavior of their courtier cousins.

In contrast, Anne's brothers, Henry (1652–1712) and James (1664–1695), were both in the royal navy and were both very much involved with the court. Henry, who is mentioned in Dryden's ode on Anne, entered the navy as a volunteer in 1666; he rose quickly through the ranks to the position of admiral, in part, Samuel Pepys seemed to feel, because he was conducting an affair with Charles's former mistress, the powerful Duchess of Castlemaine.[71] About Anne's younger brother, James, less is known: he followed his brother to sea, served with distinction in many campaigns, and died in battle. There is no record of his having married, nor what education either of Anne's brothers received prior to joining the navy. Henry died at his home in St. Albans, not far away from Wheathampstead, which again suggests that this branch of the Killigrew family was not entirely London-based. It is from Henry's will that we have learned the titles of some of Anne's paintings, which he owned but which have subsequently disappeared.[72]

Anne Killigrew's Writings and Paintings

What we presently know about Anne Killigrew's careers as a writer and a painter come from incomplete surviving records. However, as is frequently true with the recovery of texts by and about early modern women, more pieces of evidence are still being found. Prior to 2009, no manuscripts of Killigrew's poetry were known to exist; with the cataloging of the Evelyn family papers at the British Library, five poems (discussed below) have emerged from that collection. A "new" poem about Anne Killigrew, the anagram by Wodehouse, was only recently discovered in the Brotherton Collection at the University of Leeds, in part because of the digitalization of that library's manuscript holdings.

Thus the key source of information we have about Killigrew as a poet comes from the printed collection of her verse, *Poems* (1686).

71. J. K. Laughton, "Killigrew, Henry (c. 1652–1712)," rev. J. D. Davies, *ODNB*.

72. George Vertue, *Notebooks*, ed. K. Esdaile and H. M. Hake, 6 vols. Walpole Society, 18, 20, 22, 24, 26, 30 (Oxford: Clarendon Press, 1930–55); 2:58; Cust and Baker, "Notes," 112–13, 116.

The title page uses a line from Martial's *Epigrams* IV: "*Immodicis brevis est aetas, & rara Senectus,*" "To unwonted worth comes life but short, and rarely old age." It was the same epigram that the poet Abraham Cowley had used for his 1663 poem "On the Death of Mr. William Harvey" and John Dryden had invoked in his ode "On the Death of Mr. Oldham." It expresses the sentiment that those who are unusually gifted rarely have a long life, and is a lament that the early display of talent did not have the time to ripen and mature.

The volume was licensed for publication in September of 1685, only three months after her death. As the note heading the final three poems in the volume suggests, her grieving father collected his daughter's loose papers and had them printed, using an engraving of one of her self-portraits for its frontispiece. There is no indication that Anne Killigrew herself had left her papers in a form anticipating that they would be published. Instead, the contents of the volume illustrate her participation in what I have termed "social authorship," the serious pursuit of literary excellence shared with a select audience of readers using the medium of circulating handwritten copies.[73] This can be seen most clearly in poems such as "To my Lord Colrane, In Answer to his Complemental Verses sent me under the Name of Cleanor," and "Upon the saying that my Verses were made by another." This last poem also reveals some of the complicated dynamics of circulating one's writings in manuscript form: even though Killigrew and those with whom she is exchanging poems follow the tradition best seen in Katherine Philips and her "Society of Friendship" with its use of pastoral pennames helping to create a sense of a friendly but exclusive group of readers, in fact, once a manuscript left the author's hands, he or she could not completely control readers' responses to it.[74] Killigrew mentions Philips in this poem as an exemplar of the woman poet, but

73. Margaret J. M. Ezell, "The Posthumous Publication of Women's Manuscripts and the History of Authorship," in *Women's Writing and the Circulation of Ideas: Manuscript Publication in England, 1550–1800*, ed. George Justice and Nathan Tinker (Cambridge: Cambridge University Press, 2002), 121–36. See Harold Love, *Scribal Publication in Seventeenth-Century England* (Oxford: Oxford University Press, 1993) for discussion of professional and other scribal productions and their circulation.

74. For Katherine Philips and her use of manuscript circulation practices, see Elizabeth H. Hageman and Andrea Sununu, "'More Copies of It Abroad than I Could Have Imagin'd': Further Manuscript Texts of Katherine Philips, 'The Matchless Orinda,'" *English Manuscript*

in her own situation, Killigrew laments that her readers, unlike Philips's, fail to recognize or reward her verses.[75]

There is little question but that Killigrew took her writing and her painting seriously. She was skilled enough to be permitted to paint the portraits of the future king and queen, and those portraits remained in the royal collection long after their sitters had gone into exile. Although she was described by John Dryden in his ode as "Art she had none," suggesting that her verses were natural and spontaneous effusions rather than the product of training or craft, the writings that have survived demonstrate her engagement with perfecting her verse and her commitment to poetry as an art, one requiring not only technique but also inspiration. "Ah that some pitying *Muse* would now inspire / My frozen style with a Poetic fire," she hopes in the opening of her early attempt at epic in "Alexandreis." Likewise, in her poem "Upon the saying that my Verses were made by another," she echoes that sentiment: "Next Heaven my Vows to thee (O Sacred *Muse*!) / I offer'd up, nor didst thou them refuse. / . . . / An Undivided Sacrifice I'll lay / Upon thine Altar, Soul and Body pay." Her verses self-consciously recognize her limitations as she struggles to find a voice worthy of her subject, but they also declare her belief that sometimes perfect meter and smooth, pretty harmonies are not always appropriate or the most effective way to convey her meaning. In "Love, the Soul of Poetry," the early verses of the young poet "Alexis," written when "His Muse in Low, but Graceful Numbers walk't, / . . . / But never aim'd at any noble Flight: / The Herds, the Groves, the gentle purling Streams, / Adorn'd his Song, and were his highest Themes"; but when touched by "Love," the poet "With Vigor flies, where late he crept along, / And Acts Divine, in a Diviner Song, / Commits to the eternal Trump of Fame." Likewise in "The Discontent," an ode on the vanity of human wishes, Killigrew instructs her muse to "take here no Care, my *Muse*, / Nor

---

Studies, 1100–1700 5 (1995): 127–69 and Peter Beal, *In Praise of Scribes: Manuscripts and Their Makers in Seventeenth-Century England* (Oxford: Oxford University Press, 1998).

75. For a discussion of the possibilities of rivalries within manuscript circles, see Margaret Ezell, "Late Seventeenth-Century Women Poets and the Anxiety of Attribution," in *Women and the Poem in Seventeenth-Century England: Inheritance, Circulation, Exchange*, ed. Susan Wiseman (Manchester: University of Manchester Press, forthcoming).

ought of Art or Labor use / . . . / The ruggeder my Measures run when read, / They'll livelier paint th'unequal Paths fond Mortals tread."

Killigrew's collected poems show her attempts at a fairly wide range of poetic forms that were popular during the latter part of the seventeenth century. She wrote occasional verses to particular people about specific events in their lives, such as to Queen Catherine on her birthday and to a young wife whose husband has gone abroad. She wrote a few lyrics, notably one addressed to the Duchess of Grafton as "Alinda," signifying the duchess's association with Killigrew's group of readers. She also experimented in her longer poems with the new form of the Pindaric ode, a form typically used to frame a meditation on a serious subject using irregular lines and stanzas, made popular in England by Abraham Cowley in the 1660s and raised to its height by John Dryden (with some critics such as Samuel Johnson in the eighteenth century citing Dryden's ode on Killigrew as the exemplar of the form).

Her four epigrams are the nucleus of several poems commenting on contemporary manners and morals. As we have seen, epigrams were her father's preferred poetic form with their clever, incisive analysis of human character and motive. The four epigrams in the published volume exist in a manuscript copy that also includes her poem "To the Queen," and this manuscript was found in the papers of John Evelyn's father-in-law, Sir Richard Browne.[76] There are some slight variants found between the manuscript and printed text. In the second epigram on Billinda, concerning the hypocrisy of the wanton lady when her lover switches his attentions to the chaste Marcella, Marcella's name is given as "Mamurra," and the title of the third epigram has been amplified to be "On a Concealed Atheist." Such differences are small, but they are in keeping with the practices of social authorship, in which the copyist might make alterations to make the poem fit a different person or audience.[77] Like many poets and moral-

76. London, British Library, Add. MS 78233, fols. 128r–30v.

77. See Ezell, *Social Authorship and the Advent of Print* (Baltimore: Johns Hopkins University Press, 1999), Chapter 1, Beal, *In Praise of Scribes*, Chapter 1, and Elizabeth Scott-Baumann, "'Shifting dress': The Commonplacing of Katherine Philips's Poetry," paper presented at the Warwick University Symposium "Female Commonplace Books and Miscellanies," July 22, 2011.

ists, Killigrew sees the desire for wealth and prestige as the primary cause of human unhappiness; her short poem "Extemporary Counsel given to a Young Gallant in a Frolic" is clearly directed at one of her courtier acquaintances caught up in dueling and amorous intrigues when it urges, "As you are Young, if you'll be also Wise" to "Believe you then are truly Brave and Bold, / To Beauty when no Slave, and less to Gold."

She also makes extensive use of pastoral themes and characters in several of her poems. Killigrew is particularly drawn to pastoral dialogues, where multiple speakers present different opinions about love and human happiness. As critics have observed, the pastoral, with its idealized society and landscape can also serve as a means for a poet to reflect on the conditions of their own society. She also wrote several poems about her paintings on biblical subjects. As Paula Backscheider notes, however, Killigrew's rendition of biblical topics can be dark and dangerous, not because of women's vulnerabilities, but because of powerful women who work together. In her poem about her now missing painting *Herodias's Daughter presenting to her Mother St. John's Head in a Charger*, Killigrew has Salome presenting the head of John declaring, "Behold, dear Mother, who was late our Fear, / Disarm'd and Harmless, I present you here."[78] The daughter has defended her mother; through her charming of Herod with her dancing, she has won her prize, St. John's head. As she presents it to her mother, the once threatening prophet has become a conventional subdued lover: "As Lovers use, he gazes on my Face, / With Eyes that languish, as they sued for Grace; / Wholly subdu'd by my Victorious Charms."

Likewise, even more unusual than Killigrew's turn to biblical topics or pastoral motifs was her early attempt at epic. She chose as her topic the meeting between Alexander the Great and the Amazon Queen Thalestris.[79] According to her original editor's note, presumably by her father, she abandoned the poem and left it in a fragmentary state, feeling that she needed more mature talents before completing it; this fragment of "Alexandreis," however, highlights that from an early

78. Paula R. Backscheider, *Eighteenth-Century Women Poets and Their Poetry* (Baltimore: Johns Hopkins University Press, 2005), 163.

79. On Killigrew's use of warrior women, see Michael Rex, "The Heroines' Revolt: English Women Writing Epic Poetry, 1654–1789" (PhD diss., Wayne State University, 1998).

age as a writer, Killigrew knew the conventions of the genre and was ambitious to write a female form of the epic. Amazon queens recur in other of her poems as well, along with the figure of Penelope, Ulysses's wife, who not only waited patiently for him to return from the Trojan War but also held his home against suitors who would seize both it and her while he was away. It is clear that for Killigrew the classics were not only stories about lustful gods and their hapless females, but also about women who commanded armies and assisted cities, and about real wives and queens such as Queen Catherine, whose virtue never wavered even during the most difficult of times.

Afterlife of Killigrew's Works

Although Killigrew herself declared in "An Epitaph on Herself," "When I am Dead, few Friends attend my Hearse, / And for a Monument, I leave my VERSE," her character and life as much as her poetry has been the subject of later generation's attention. Several contemporary poets such as John Chatwin and Edmund Wodehouse (whose verses about Killigrew are included in Appendix 1), comment on both her exemplary life and her talents as a poet. Dryden masterfully uses Killigrew in his "Ode," focusing attention on her youth and innocence: his "Youngest Virgin-Daughter of the Skies" contrasts and condemns "this lubrique and adult'rate age" and its "steaming Ordures of the Stage." His insistence that Killigrew's was a heavenly voice that did not need technical artifice drew attention to the very real roughness of her compositions. Her volume of poetry was not reprinted, but eight of her poems were anthologized in the eighteenth century in *Poems by Eminent Ladies* (1755). The biographical entry on her in this anthology quotes Dryden's "Ode," and following a description of her upbringing by Anthony à Wood states that "Her superior genius being improved by a polite education, she made a great proficiency in the arts of Poetry and Painting." The entry concludes with the prediction that "had it pleased Providence to have prolonged her life, she might probably have rivaled the greatest masters in each."[80] This anthology, however, perpetuates the image of Killigrew, along with the other women poets

80. George Colman and Bonnell Thornton, eds., *Poems by Eminent Ladies*, 2 vols. (London, 1755), 2:2.

it includes, as poetically untrained: "most of these Ladies (like many of our greatest male writers) were more indebted to nature for their success, than to education; and it was therefore thought better to omit those pieces, which too plainly betrayed the want of learning."[81] The source for the biographical entry on her was undoubtedly George Ballard's *Memoirs of Several Ladies of Great Britain* (1752), which it echoes closely.[82]

Even though seemingly damned with this faint praise, there was sufficient interest in Killigrew as a Restoration poet for two facsimile editions of her *Poems* to be produced in the twentieth century, and she has figured steadily in literary criticism concerned with women writers.[83] Likewise, there has been a renewal of interest in Killigrew as an artist, especially as a court portrait painter.[84] Killigrew appears in Germaine Greer's early study of women artists, *The Obstacle Race* (1979), and both Killigrew's art and poetry are treated sympathetically and at length in Carol Barash's *English Women's Poetry, 1649–1714: Politics, Community, and Linguistic Authority* (1996).[85] More recently, there is a growing body of criticism interested in her life and writings from a feminist and political perspective.[86]

81. Colman and Thornton, *Poems*, vol. 1, sig. A2v.

82. George Ballard, *Memoirs of Several Ladies of Great Britain*, ed. Ruth Perry (Detroit: Wayne State University Press, 1985), 304–9.

83. *Poems (1686)*, with introduction by Richard Morton (Gainesville, FL: Scholar's Facsimiles and Reprints, 1967); and *Anne Killigrew*, with introduction by Patricia Hoffmann, The Early Modern Englishwoman: A Facsimile Library of Essential Works, Series 2, Published Writings, 1641–1700, pt. 2, vol. 5 (Aldershot, UK: Ashgate Publishing, 2003).

84. Barash, *English Women's Poetry*, has in an appendix a list of Killigrew's paintings and their locations, although at that time she was unaware of the second painting of an unknown woman held at Berkeley Castle, as well as those paintings for which we have some records but whose current location is unknown.

85. Germaine Greer, *The Obstacle Race* (London: Picador, 1979), 281, 283–84; Barash, *English Women's Poetry*, chapter 4.

86. See Margaret Anne Doody, *The Daring Muse: Augustan Poetry Reconsidered* (Cambridge: Cambridge University Press, 1985), 254–55. Good overviews of previous criticism on Killigrew as well as an appreciation of her pastoral poems can be found in Brian Eliot, "'To Love Have Prov'd a Foe': Virginity, Virtue, and Love's Dangers in Anne Killigrew's Pastoral Dialogues," *Restoration: Studies in English Literary Culture, 1660–1700* 33, no.1 (2009): 27–41 and Rafael Vélez-Núñez, "Broken Emblems: Anne Killigrew's Pictorial Poetry," in

Concerning Killigrew's place in the poets of the Restoration period, the poet to whom John Dryden links Killigrew is Katherine Philips, and she was the poet Killigrew herself wrote about with admiration in her poem "Upon the saying that my Verses were made by another." Both women wrote poems confronting the values of their times and both wrote of their desire for a retreat from it with like-minded souls; both were members of groups of writers circulating their works in manuscript rather than seeking immediate publication. And, of course, both died young from smallpox, as highlighted by Dryden and numerous other contemporary commentators. However, it is also instructive to put Killigrew in the company of that other versifying maid of honor in the court of Mary of Modena, Anne Finch, Countess of Winchilsea, as Carol Barash's study does, and also to contrast her with the now most well-known woman writer of that period, the commercial poet and dramatist Aphra Behn. Finch, too, was not of the temper or disposition to become a maid of honor who would be mentioned in satires and lampoons, and her later poetry treats seriously the value of a retired, contemplative life and possesses a satiric streak that one also finds in Killigrew. Behn, unlike Killigrew, earned her living from her writing, publishing successful comedies as well as translations, novels, and miscellany editions. Behn, although a generation older than Killigrew, moved along the theatrical fringes of the court, was a friend of Rochester's, and was a staunch admirer of both Charles II and his brother James, dedicating several works to members of the royal family. Although very much part of the libertine world of the theater, Behn also cast her satiric eye on the rakish behavior of the male courtiers, turning the exploits of the hero of Thomas Killigrew's 1650s drama *Thomaso The Wanderer* into the ambiguous portrait of Willmore in *The Rover, or The Banished Cavaliers* (1677): as critics have noted, Willmore is depicted in the two-part play more as a drunken, ineffectual fortune-hunter than as a dashing hero.

The difference between Killigrew, Philips, Finch, and Behn, however, is that Philips died when she was thirty-two, still quite young, but fully a decade after her first poems began appearing in print and after *Pompey*, her translation of Pierre Corneille's *La Mort de Pompée*,

---

Re-Shaping the Genres: Restoration Women Writers, ed. Xenón Luis-Martinez and Jorge Figueroa-Dorrego (Berne: Peter Lang, 2003), 49–66.

had been successfully staged in Dublin in 1663. Likewise, Finch did not publish her poetry until the 1690s, and her collected verse was not published until 1713. Behn was successful at earning her living through writing for almost twenty years. This meant that both Philips and Finch enjoyed a considerably longer period as social poets than Killigrew, circulating their work among sophisticated readers and critics before their verses were presented to the general reading public in printed single-author volumes. Behn was a seasoned commercial writer, whose plays and novels enjoyed a steady contemporary readership and whose success had gained her a place in the professional literary world of the London theater. The single posthumously published volume of Killigrew's poems, therefore, should be viewed not so much as a final polished product against these other writers, but instead as a record of the aspirations and poetic vision of a developing young artist, one finding another voice in the world of Restoration politics and poetics.

Note on the Text

Anne Killigrew's poems were published in a single edition. It was licensed by Roger L'Estrange in September 1685, only three months after her death, and advertised in *The Observator* on November 2, 1685, although its title page gives the publication date as 1686. The volume used for the preparation of this edition is held at the Folger Shakespeare Library (shelfmark K422 Cage).

In order to make this edition more readable for a modern audience, the following modernizations of the text have been made. Line numbers have been added for all the verse. Spelling has been regularized to conform to modern American usage, except in cases in which the meter, rhyme, or sound of the lines would be affected. All contractions and abbreviations which do not affect the meter have been expanded, such as "ye" and "yt" rendered as "the" and "that," with the exception of "&" found in the Latin verse. Pronouns which Killigrew's text printed as "her self" or "them selves" have been closed up according to modern spelling. The seventeenth-century poetic contractions "o're," "ne're," and "e're" have been changed to "o'er," "ne'er," and "e'er" for "over," "never," and "ever" to assist modern readers and yet maintain the meter. In the dialogue poems, the abbreviations of speakers' names have been expanded to their full names and italicized for ease of reading. Other punctuation including the use of italics and capital letters has been retained as found in the original volume, except in the titles of the poems, where periods have been removed and title words printed in all capitals or varying fonts have been regularized. Poems with the same title are distinguished by the addition of (1), (2), and (3). Where needed, appropriate apostrophes have been added to possessive nouns. The names of characters within the poems have been regularized. In the poems about Anne Killigrew, I have regularized the spelling of her first name. The *Oxford English Dictionary* is the source for word definitions in the glosses, and the King James Version of the Bible is the source cited for the biblical allusions. Modern typesetting differs from that in the seventeenth-century, but every effort has been made to preserve the original style of the line indentions of the verses.

Appendix 1 contains poems written about Anne Killigrew. Three of these, "The Publisher to the Reader," "To the Pious Memory Of the Accomplisht Young Lady Mrs. Anne Killigrew" by John Dryden, and "The Epitaph Engraved on her Tomb" with its translation, were printed as front matter in Killigrew's *Poems*. The other three, "To the Pious Memory of Mrs. Anne Killigrew. A Pindaric" by John Chatwin, "On the Death of the Truly Virtuous Mrs. Anne Killigrew, who was Related to my (Deceased) Wife" by "E. E.," and "Anagram on Mistress Anne Killigrew" by Edmund Wodehouse, are found in single manuscript copies. Chatwin's was preserved in a fair copy in his hand in Bodleian Library, MS Rawl. poet. 94, fols. 149–52, and has been published by Stuart Gillespie in "Another Pindaric Ode 'To the Pious Memory of Mrs. Anne Killigrew,'" *Restoration: Studies in English Literary Culture, 1660–1700* 20, (1996): 31–35, and by Carol Barash as an appendix to *English Women's Poetry, 1649–1714: Politics, Community, and Linguistic Authority* (Oxford: Oxford University Press, 1996), 301–3. The poem by "E. E." identified as being by Edmond Elys, is a manuscript inscription on the flyleaf of the edition of Killigrew's *Poems* held by the Alexander Turnbull Library in Wellington, New Zealand and was published by Richard Morton in his facsimile edition of the *Poems (1686)* (Gainesville, FL: Scholars' Facsimiles and Reprints, 1967), xi–xii. The final poem in this appendix by

Edmund Wodehouse is part of a large manuscript miscellany held at the University of Leeds, Brotherton Library, MS Lt 40, fol. 124v, whose contents date between 1664 and 1715.

Appendix 2 contains poems not by Killigrew that were published at the end of the volume of her verse. Their place in Killigrew's volume is explained by the publisher with the note, "These Three following ODES being found among Mrs. Killigrew's Paper, I was willing to Print though none of hers." They are presently unattributed, but they are included in this volume to provide examples of what types of subjects and verse forms were in use among those poets whom she was reading and with whom Killigrew was exchanging her verses.

Appendix 3 includes poems written about the death of Killigrew's aunt, Anne Killigrew Kirke, who drowned in 1641 and whose loss was the subject of several poems by her contemporaries. These provide a contextualization for the poem Killigrew herself wrote on this subject.

Appendix 4 includes a sampling of contemporary verse by the Restoration libertine poet John Wilmot, Earl of Rochester, and an anonymous satire on the court "An Heroic Poem" (c. 1681). These are intended to give readers a sense of Restoration courtier verse, and the ways in which the young women of the court figured in contemporary lyrics and satires.

Alexandreis[1]

I Sing the Man[2] that never Equal knew,
Whose Mighty Arms all *Asia* did subdue,
Whose Conquests through the spacious World do ring,
That City-Razer, King-destroying King,
Who o'er the Warlike *Macedons* did Reign,
And worthily the Name of *Great* did gain.
This is the Prince (if Fame you will believe,
To ancient Story any credit give)
Who when the Globe of Earth he had subdu'd,
With Tears the easy Victory pursu'd;
Because that no more Worlds there were to win,
No further Scene to act his Glories in.

Ah that some pitying *Muse* would now inspire
My frozen style with a Poetic fire,
And Raptures worthy of his Matchless Fame,
Whose Deeds I sing, whose never fading Name
Long as the world shall fresh and deathless last,
No less to future Ages, than the past.
Great my presumption is, I must confess,

1. Also the name of the medieval Latin epic poem by a twelfth-century French writer named Walter of Châtillon. It is part of a body of texts called the Alexander romances that were extremely popular in medieval English and consisted of legends about the life and deeds of Alexander the Great (356–323 BC), the Greek king of Macedonia, who before his death created the largest empire ever known, spanning Asia and the Persian empire. Episode eight of Châtillon's poem recounts Alexander's meeting with Thalestris, queen of the Amazons. His source, *The Ten Books of Quintus Curtius Rufus: Containing, the Life and Death of Alexander the Great*, was first translated by Robert Codrington in 1652 and enjoyed numerous reprints during Killigrew's lifetime, notably in 1673 and 1674.

2. An allusion to the opening line of Virgil's epic, *The Aeneid*: "Arms and the man I sing, who, forced by fate / And haughty Juno's unrelenting hate, / Expelled and exiled, left the Trojan shore." John Dryden, *The Works of Virgil Containing his Pastorals, Georgics and Aeneis* (London, 1697), 201.

But if I thrive, my Glory's ne're the less;
Nor will it from his Conquests derogate[3]
A Female Pen his Acts did celebrate.
If thou O *Muse* wilt thy assistance give,
Such as made *Naso* and great *Maro* live,[4]
With him whom *Melas's* fertile Banks did bear,[5]
Live, though their Bodies dust and ashes are;
Whose Laurels[6] were not fresher, than their Fame
Is now, and will forever be the same.
If the like favor thou wilt grant to me,
O Queen of Verse,[7] I'll not ungrateful be,
My choicest hours to thee I'll Dedicate,
'Tis thou shalt rule, 'tis thou shalt be my Fate.
But if Coy Goddess thou shalt this deny,
And from my humble suit disdaining fly,
I'll stoop and beg no more, since I know this,
Writing of him, I cannot write amiss:
His lofty Deeds will raise each feeble line,
And God-like Acts will make my Verse Divine.

'Twas at the time the golden Sun doth rise,
And with his Beams enlights the azure skies,
When lo a Troop in Silver Arms drew near,
The glorious Sun did ne're so bright appear;
Dire Scarlet Plumes adorn'd their haughty Crests,
And crescent Shields did shade their shining Breasts;
Down from their shoulders hung a Panther's Hide,
A Bow and Quiver rattled by their side;
Their hands a knotty well-tried Spear did bear,
Jocund they seem'd, and quite devoid of fear.

3. Lessen the authority or impair the strength.

4. The Roman poets Ovid (43 BC–17 AD) and Virgil (70–19 BC), respectively Publius Ovidius Naso and Publius Vergilius Maro.

5. Alexander; he crossed the river Melus during his conquest of Persia.

6. In ancient Greece the laurel wreath was a symbol of victory and status, given to the winner in a competition.

7. The muse Killigrew is invoking, perhaps Calliope, the muse of epic poetry.

These warlike Virgins[8] were, that do reside
Near *Thermodon's* smooth Banks and verdant side,
The Plains of *Themiscyre* their Birth do boast,
Thalestris[9] now did head the beauteous Host;
She emulating that Illustrious Dame,
Who to the aid of *Troy* and *Priam* came,[10]
And her who the *Retulian* Prince[11] did aid,
Though dearly both for their Assistance paid.
But fear she scorn'd, nor the like fate did dread,
Her Host she often to the field had led,
As oft in Triumph had return'd again,
Glory she only sought for all her pain.

This Martial Queen had heard how loudly fame,
Echo'd our Conqueror's redoubted[12] Name,
Her Soul his Conduct and his Courage fir'd,
To see the Hero she so much admir'd;
And to *Hyrcania*[13] for this cause she went,
Where *Alexander* (wholly then intent
On Triumphs and such Military sport)
At Truce with War held both his Camp and Court.
And while before the Town she did attend
Her Messengers return, she saw ascend
A cloud of Dust, that cover'd all the sky,
And still at every pause there struck her eye.

8. In Greek mythology, the Amazons, a female warrior race whose capital Themiscyre was on the river Thermodon.

9. The queen of the Amazons, who is said to have brought three hundred women warriors to meet with Alexander.

10. In the *Aeneid*, the Amazon Queen Penthesilea comes to the aid of King Priam of Troy after the death of the hero Hector; she fights well but is ultimately defeated by Achilles.

11. In the *Aeneid*, Turnus is the king of the Rutuli; a hotheaded and willful character, he is the chief human antagonist for its hero Aeneas; Camilla is the maiden warrior leader of the Volsi who, in the resulting war between the Trojans and the Latins told in Book XI, comes to help defend the city and dies bravely on the battlefield.

12. Revered, commanding respect.

13. Province in ancient Persia invaded by Alexander in 330 BC.

The interrupted Beams of Burnisht Gold,
As dust the Splendor hid, or did unfold;
Loud Neighings of the Steeds, and Trumpets sound
Fill'd all the Air, and echo'd from the ground:
The gallant *Greeks* with a brisk March drew near,
And their great Chief did at their Head appear.
And now come up to th'*Amazonian* Band,
They made a Halt and a respectful Stand:
And both the Troops (with like amazement strook)[14]
Did each on other with deep silence look.
Th'Heroic Queen (whose high pretence to War
Cancell'd the bashful Laws and nicer Bar
Of Modesty, which did her Sex restrain)
First boldly did advance before her Train,
And thus she spake, "All but a God in Name,
And that a debt Time owes unto thy Fame."

This was the first Essay of this young Lady in Poetry, but finding the Task she had undertaken hard, she laid it by till Practice and more time should make her equal to so great a Work.

To the Queen[15]

As those who pass the *Alps* do say,
The Rocks which first oppose their way,
And so amazing-High do show,
By fresh Ascents appear but low,
And when they come unto the last,
They scorn the dwarfish Hills th'ave passed.

So though my *Muse* at her first flight,
Thought she had chose the greatest height,

14. Struck.

15. Catherine of Braganza (1638–1705), wife of England's King Charles II.

And (imp'd[16] with *Alexander's* Name)[17]
Believ'd there was no further Fame:
Behold, an Eye wholly Divine
Vouchsaf'd upon my Verse to Shine!
And from that time I'gan to treat
With Pity him the World call'd *Great*;
To smile at his exalted Fate,
Unequal (though Gigantic) State.
I saw that Pitch was not sublime,
Compar'd with this which now I climb;
His Glories sunk, and were unseen,
When once appear'd the Heav'n-born Queen:
Victories, Laurels, Conquer'd Kings,
Took place among inferior things.

Now surely I shall reach the Clouds,
For none besides such Virtue shrouds:
Having scal'd this with holy Strains,
Nought higher but the Heaven remains!
No more I'll Praise on them bestow,
Who to ill Deeds their Glories owe;
Who build their *Babels*[18] of Renown,
Upon the poor oppressed Crown,
Whole Kingdoms do depopulate,
To raise a Proud and short-Liv'd State:
I prize no more such Frantic Might,
Than his that did with Wind-Mills Fight:[19]
No, give me Prowess, that with Charms
Of Grace and Goodness, not with Harms,
Erects a Throne i'th' inward Parts,
And Rules men's Wills, but with their Hearts;

16. Engrafted, applied to.

17. "The Alexandreis" was Killigrew's early attempt at writing an epic.

18. The tower of Babel was built by man in a prideful attempt to create a structure that could reach heaven (Genesis 11:4–9).

19. Don Quixote, the character in Cervantes's mock epic story who is so carried away with stories of chivalry he challenges windmills to a duel.

Who with Piety and Virtue thus
Propitiates God, and Conquers us.
O that now like *Araunah* here,
Altars of Praises I could rear,[20]
Suiting her worth, which might be seen
Like a Queen's Present, to a Queen!

"Alone she stands for Virtue's Cause,
When all decry, upholds her Laws:
When to Banish her is the Strife,
Keeps her unexil'd in her Life;
Guarding her matchless Innocence
From Storms of boldest Impudence;
Inspite of all the Scoffs and Rage,
And Persecutions of the Age,
Owns Virtue's Altar, feeds the Flame,
Adores her much-derided Name;
While impiously her hands they tie,
Loves her in her Captivity;
Like *Perseus* saves her, when she stands
Expos'd to the *Leviathans*.[21]
So did bright Lamps once live in Urns,[22]
So Camphor in the water burns,[23]
So *Ætna's* Flames[24] do ne'er go out,
Though Snows do freeze her head without."

20. David erected an altar on the threshing floor of Araunah to praise God and atone for his sins (2 Samuel 24:18–25).

21. In Greek myth, the hero Perseus rescued Andromeda, chained to a rock, from a sea monster; Killigrew expands the story by having her threatened by Leviathans, sea monsters most typically found in Hebrew poetry.

22. References to ever-burning lamps were frequently found in medieval and early modern texts devoted to explaining magical and alchemical phenomenon; Sir Thomas Browne in his very popular book *Pseudodoxia Epidemica* (1646), which was frequently reprinted in the later part of the seventeenth century, mentions them.

23. Camphor is so flammable that it continues to burn on the surface of water.

24. Mount Etna in Sicily is the highest mountain in Italy and, since classical times, a highly active volcano. It had a massive eruption in 1669, about which many accounts were written in both Italian and English.

How dares bold Vice unmasked walk,
And like a Giant proudly stalk?
When Virtue's so exalted seen,
Arm'd and Triumphant in the Queen?
How dares its Ulcerous Face appear,
When Heavenly Beauty is so near?
But so when God was close at hand,
And the bright Cloud did threatning stand
(In sight of *Israel*) on the Tent,
They on in their Rebellion went.[25]

O that I once so happy were,
To find a nearer Shelter there!
'Til then poor Dove, I wandering fly
Between the Deluge and the Sky:
'Til then I Mourn, but do not sing,
And oft shall plunge my wearied wing:
If her bless'd hand vouchsafe the Grace,
I'th' Ark with her to give a place,
I safe from danger shall be found,
When Vice and Folly others drown'd.[26]

A Pastoral Dialogue (1)

Dorinda. Sabæan[27] Perfumes fragrant Roses bring,
With all the Flowers that Paint the gaudy Spring:
Scatter them all in young *Alexis's* way,
With all that's sweet and (like himself) that's Gay.

Alexis. Immortal Laurels and as lasting Praise,

25. The rebellion of Korah and his followers against Moses and Aaron resulted in God appearing in a cloud as a warning (Numbers 16:42).

26. Noah sends a dove from the sanctuary of the Ark to see if the flood waters which have destroyed all things on earth have receded (Genesis 8:8–12).

27. From Sabea, an ancient area of Yemen in Arabia, noted for its spices.

Crown the Divine *Dorinda's* matchless Lays[28]:
May all Hearts stoop, where mine would gladly yield,
Had not *Lycoris* prepossest the Field.

Dorinda. Would my *Alexis* meet my noble Flame,
In all *Ausonia*[29] neither Youth nor Dame,
Should so renown'd in Deathless Numbers shine,
As thy exalted Name should do in mine.

Alexis. He'll need no Trophy nor ambitious Hearse,
Who shall be honour'd by *Dorinda's* Verse;[30]
But where it is inscrib'd, *That here doth lie*
Lycoris's Love. That Fame can never die.

Dorinda. On *Tiber's* Bank I *Thyrsis*[31] did espy,
And by his side did bright *Lycoris* lie;
She Crown'd his Head, and Kist his amorous Brow,
Ah Poor *Alexis*! Ah then where wer't thou?

Alexis. When thou saw'st that, I ne'r had seen my Fair,
And what pass'd then ought not to be my Care;
I liv'd not then, but first began to be,
When I *Lycoris* Lov'd, and she Lov'd me.

Dorinda. Ah choose a Faith, a Faith that's like thine own,
A Virgin Love, a Love that's newly blown:
'Tis not enough a Maiden's Heart is chaste,
It must be Single, and not once mis-plac't.

Alexis. Thus do our Priests of Heavenly Pastures tell,
Eternal Groves, all Earthly, that excel:

28. Short poems to be sung.

29. Ancient name for the region in middle and south Italy, and in poetry often used to describe all of Italy.

30. Lycoris will not need a fancy monument if Dorinda writes about him.

31. The Tiber is a major river in Italy that flows through Rome to the sea; Thyrsis is a shepherd in Virgil's *Seventh Eclogue* and Theocritus's first *Bucolic* who is noted for his singing.

And think to wean us from our Loves below,
By dazzling Objects which we cannot know.

On Death

Tell me thou safest End of all our Woe,
Why wretched Mortals do avoid thee so:
Thou gentle drier o'th' afflicted's Tears,
Thou noble ender of the Coward's Fears;
Thou sweet Repose to Lovers' sad despair,
Thou Calm t'Ambition's rough Tempestuous Care.
If in regard of Bliss thou wert a Curse,
And then the Joys of Paradise art worse;
Yet after Man from his first Station fell,
And God from *Eden Adam* did expel,
Thou wert no more an Evil, but Relief;
The Balm and Cure to ev'ry Human Grief:
Through thee (what Man had forfeited before)
He now enjoys, and ne'er can lose it more.
No subtle Serpents in the Grave betray,
Worms on the Body there, not Soul do prey;
No Vice there Tempts, no Terrors there afright,
No Coz'ning[32] Sin affords a false delight:
No vain Contentions do that Peace annoy,
No fierce Alarms break the lasting Joy.

Ah since from thee so many Blessings flow,
Such real Good as Life can never know;
Come when thou wilt, in thy afrighting'st Dress,
Thy Shape shall never make thy Welcome less.
Thou mayst to Joy, but ne'er to Fear give Birth,
Thou Best, as well as Certain'st thing on Earth.
Fly thee? May Travelers then fly their Rest,
And hungry Infants fly the profer'd Breast.
No, those that faint and tremble at thy Name,

32. Cheating.

Fly from their Good on a mistaken Fame.
Thus Childish fear did *Israel* of old
From Plenty and the Promis'd Land withhold;
They fancy'd Giants, and refus'd to go,
When *Canaan* did with Milk and Honey flow.[33]

First Epigram
Upon being Contented with a Little

We deem them moderate, but *Enough* implore,
What barely will suffice, and ask no more:
Who say, "(O Jove) *a competency give,*
Neither in Luxury, or Want we'd live."
But what is that, which these *Enough* do call?
If both the *Indies* unto some should fall,
Such Wealth would yet *Enough* but only be,
And what they'd term not Want, or Luxury.
Among the Suits *O Jove*, my humbler take;
A little give, I that Enough will make.

The Second Epigram
On Billinda

Wanton *Billinda* loudly does complain,
I've chang'd my Love of late into disdain:
Calls me unconstant, 'cause I now adore
The chaste *Marcella*, that lov'd her before.
Sin or Dishonor, me as well may blame,
That I repent, or do avoid a shame.

33. When Moses sent spies into Canaan, they returned reporting it full of milk and honey but inhabited by the sons of Anak who were giants (Numbers 13:27–33).

The Third Epigram
On an Atheist

Posthumus[34] boasts he does not Thunder fear,
And for this cause would Innocent appear;
That in his Soul no Terror he does feel,
At threatn'd Vultures, or *Ixion's* Wheel,[35]
Which fright the Guilty: But when *Fabius* told
What Acts 'gainst Murder lately were enrol'd,
'Gainst Incest, Rapine, —— straight upon the Tale
His Color chang'd, and *Posthumus* grew pale.
His Impious Courage had no other Root,
But that the Villain, Atheist was to boot.[36]

The Fourth Epigram
On Galla[37]

Now liquid Streams by the fierce Cold do grow
As solid as the Rocks from whence they flow;
Now *Tiber's* Banks with Ice united meet,
And its firm Stream may well be term'd its Street;
Now Vot'ries 'fore the Shrines like Statues show,
And scarce the Men from Images we know;
Now Winter's Palsy seizes ev'ry Age,
And none's so warm, but feels the Season's Rage;
Even the bright Lilies and triumphant Red

34. A word associated with death, it signifies an event occurring after a death, making this an ironic name for a character who does not believe there are any consequences or punishments for one's living actions after one has died.

35. In Greek mythology, Tityus is linked to Ixion, Sisyphus, and Tantalus, because all were punished by the gods in Tartarus; Tityus was a giant who attempted to rape Leto, the mother of Diana and Apollo and was shot by their arrows; he was sentenced to be pegged out on the ground while vultures continually tore at his liver, while Ixion was punished by Zeus for attempting to seduce Hera by being bound to a fiery wheel for eternity.

36. In addition to.

37. In classical mythology, a river nymph or female spirit, in this instance one who dwells near the river Tiber outside of Rome.

Which o'er *Corinna's* youthful cheeks are spread,
Look pale and bleak, and show a purple hew,
And Violets stain, where Roses lately grew.
   Galla alone, with wonder we behold,
Maintain her Spring, and still out-brave the Cold;
Her constant white does not to Frost give place,
Nor fresh Vermillion[38] fade upon her face:
   Sure Divine beauty in this Dame does shine?
   Not Human, one reply'd, yet not Divine.

A Farewell
To Worldly Joys

   Farewell you Unsubstantial Joys,
You Gilded Nothings, Gaudy Toys,
Too long you have my Soul misled,
Too long with Airy Diet fed:
But now my Heart you shall no more
Deceive, as you have heretofore:
For when I hear such *Sirens* sing,
Like *Ithaca's* fore-warned King,[39]
With prudent Resolution I
Will so my Will and Fancy tie,
That stronger to the Mast not he,
Than I to Reason bound will be:
And though your Witchcrafts strike my Ear,
Unhurt, like him, your Charms I'll hear.

38. Brilliant scarlet red color.

39. In the *Odyssey*, book 12, Odysseus has been warned by the witch Circe that those who hear the Sirens' song are magically enslaved by it. He has his men plug their ears and bind him to the mast of the ship so he can hear the song without being drawn to it.

The Complaint of a Lover

Seest thou yonder craggy Rock,
Whose Head o'er-looks the swelling Main,
Where never Shepherd fed his Flock,
Or careful Peasant sow'd his Grain.

No wholesome Herb grows on the same,
Or Bird of Day will on it rest;
'Tis Barren as the Hopeless Flame,
That scorches my tormented Breast.

Deep underneath a Cave does lie,
Th' entrance hid with dismal Yew,[40]
Where *Phoebus*[41] never show'd his Eye,
Or cheerful Day yet pierced through.

In that dark Melancholy Cell,[42]
(Retreat and Solace to my Woe)
Love, sad Despair, and I, do dwell,
The Springs from whence my Griefs do flow.

Treacherous Love that did appear,
(When he at first approach't my Heart)
Drest in a Garb far from severe,
Or threat'ning ought of future smart.

So Innocent those Charms then seem'd,
When *Rosalinda* first I spy'd,
Ah! Who would them have deadly deem'd?
But Flowers do often Serpents hide.

Beneath those sweets conceal'd lay,
To Love the cruel Foe, Disdain,

40. A tree, typically a symbol of sadness.

41. In classical mythology, Apollo, god of light and sun.

42. A dwelling of a single room, typically inhabited by a hermit.

With which (alas) she does repay
   My Constant and Deserving Pain.

When I in Tears have spent the Night,
   With Sighs I usher in the Sun,
Who never saw a sadder sight,
   In all the Courses he has run.

Sleep, which to others Ease does prove,
   Comes unto me, alas, in vain:
For in my Dreams I am in Love,
   And in them too she does Disdain.

Some times t'Amuse my Sorrow, I
   Unto the hollow Rocks repair,
And loudly to the *Echo* cry,
   Ah! gentle Nymph come ease my Care.[43]

Thou who, times past, a Lover wer't,
   Ah! pity me, who now am so,
And by a sense of thine own smart,
   Alleviate my Mighty Woe.

Come Flatter then, or Chide my Grief;
   Catch my last Words, and call me Fool;
Or say, she Loves, for my Relief;
   My Passion either soothe, or School.

Love, the Soul of Poetry

   When first *Alexis* did in Verse delight,
His Muse in Low, but Graceful Numbers walk't,
And now and then a little Proudly stalk't;

43. In classical mythology, Echo, a beautiful nymph cursed by Juno so that she can speak only to repeat another's words, falls in love with Narcissus. After he rejects her, she fades away in the mountain caves until only her voice is left.

But never aim'd at any noble Flight:
The Herds, the Groves, the gentle purling[44] Streams,
Adorn'd his Song, and were his highest Themes.

But Love these Thoughts, like Mists, did soon disperse,
Enlarg'd his Fancy, and set free his Muse,
Bidding him more Illustrious Subjects choose;
The Acts of Gods, and God-like Men rehearse.
From thence new Raptures did his Breast inspire,
His scarce Warm-Heart converted was to Fire.

Th' exalted Poet rais'd by this new Flame,
With Vigor flies, where late he crept along,
And Acts Divine, in a Diviner Song,
Commits to the eternal Trump[45] of Fame.
And thus *Alexis* does prove Love to be,
As the World's Soul, the Soul of Poetry.

To my Lady Berkeley, Afflicted upon her Son, My Lord Berkeley's Early Engaging in the Sea-Service[46]

So the renown'd *Ithacasian* Queen[47]
In Tears for her *Telemachus* was seen,
When leaving Home, he did attempt the Ire
Of raging Seas, to seek his absent Sire:

44. Eddying or rippling.

45. A poetic word for trumpet; the figure of Fame is traditionally represented as holding a trumpet.

46. Christiana Riccard (1639–1698), wife of John Berkeley, 1st Baron Berkeley of Stratton (bap. 1607–1678), appointed commissioner of the navy at the Restoration; their son John Berkeley, 3rd Baron Berkeley of Stratton (1663–1697), served as a volunteer in the navy between 1680 and 1684, and was appointed lieutenant of the *Bristol* on April 14, 1685.

47. In the *Odyssey*, when Odysseus leaves for the war in Troy, his wife Penelope is left at home in Ithaca with their infant son Telemachus; when the epic opens, Telemachus is of age to begin his own journeys and adventures, aided by the goddess Athena.

Such bitter Sighs her tender Breast did rend;
But had she known a God did him attend,
And would with Glory bring him safe again,
Bright Thoughts would then have dispossess't her Pain.

Ah Noblest Lady! You that her excel
In every Virtue, may in Prudence well
Suspend your Care; knowing what power befriends
Your Hopes, and what on Virtue still attends.
In bloody Conflicts he will Armor find,
In strongest Tempests he will rule the Wind,
He will through Thousand Dangers force a way,
And still Triumphant will his Charge convey.
And the All-ruling power that can act thus,
Will safe return your Dear *Telemachus.*

Alas, he was not born to live in Peace,
Souls of his Temper were not made for Ease,
Th'Ignoble only live secure from Harms,
The Generous tempt, and seek out fierce Alarms.
Huge Labors were for *Hercules* design'd,
Jason, to fetch the Golden Fleece, enjoin'd,
The *Minotaur* by Noble *Theseus* died,[48]
In vain were Valor, if it were not tried,
Should the admir'd and far-sought Diamond lie,
As in its Bed, unpolish't to the Eye,
It would be slighted like a common stone,
Its Value would be small, its Glory none.
But when't has pass'd the Wheel and Cutter's hand,[49]
Then it is meet in Monarchs' Crowns to stand.

48. Three heroes in classical mythology: Hercules was assigned twelve impossible tasks by the Oracle at Delphi to atone for killing his wife and children; Jason, the leader of the Argonauts, must capture the Golden Fleece to regain his throne; Theseus must kill the savage half-man, half-bull, the Minotaur, to stop the sacrifice of Athenian youth.

49. Tools used to shape and polish gemstones.

Upon the Noble Object of your Care
Heaven has bestow'd, of Worth, so large a share,
That unastonisht none can him behold,
Or credit all the Wonders of him told!
When others, at his Years were turning o'er,
The Acts of Heroes that had liv'd before,
Their Valor to excite, when time should fit,
He then did Things, were Worthy to be writ!
Stay'd not for Time, his Courage that out-ran
In Actions, far before in Years, a Man.
Two *French* Campaigns he boldly courted Fame,
While his Face more the Maid, than Youth became;
Add then to these a Soul so truly Mild,
Though more than Man, Obedient as a Child.
And (ah) should one Small Isle all these confine,
Virtues created through the World to shine?
Heaven that forbids, and Madam so should you;
Remember he but bravely does pursue
His Noble Father's steps; with your own Hand
Then Gird his Armor on, like him he'll stand,
His Country's Champion, and Worthy be
Of your High Virtue, and his Memory.

St. John Baptist Painted by herself in the Wilderness, with Angels appearing to him, and with a Lamb by him[50]

The Sun's my Fire, when it does shine,
The hollow Spring's my Cave of Wine,
The Rocks and Woods afford me Meat;

50. A reference to a painting by Killigrew whose current location is unknown. In the New Testament gospels, St. John foretells the coming of Christ: "In those days came John the Baptist, preaching in the wilderness of Judaea, And saying, Repent ye: for the kingdom of heaven is at hand. For this is he that was spoken of by the prophet Esaias, saying, The voice of one crying in the wilderness, Prepare ye the way of the Lord, make his paths straight. And the same John had his raiment of camel's hair, and a leathern girdle about his loins; and his meat was locusts and wild honey" (Matthew 3:1–4). In early modern paintings, he is frequently depicted with a lamb, the symbol of Christ.

This Lamb and I on one Dish eat:
The neighboring Herds my Garments send,
My Pallet the kind Earth doth lend:
Excess and Grandeur I decline,
M'Associates only are Divine.

Herodias's Daughter presenting to her Mother St. John's Head in a Charger,[51] also Painted by herself[52]

Behold, dear Mother, who was late our Fear,
Disarm'd and Harmless, I present you here;
The Tongue ty'd up, that made all *Jury*[53] quake,
And which so often did our Greatness shake;
No Terror sits upon his Awful Brow,
Where Fierceness reign'd, there Calmness triumphs now;
As Lovers use, he gazes on my Face,
With Eyes that languish, as they sued for Grace;
Wholly subdu'd by my Victorious Charms,
See how his Head reposes in my Arms.
Come, join then with me in my just Transport,
Who thus have brought the Hermit[54] to the Court.

51. A large decorative platter, typically used to display food at banquets and special occasions.

52. A reference to a painting by Killligrew whose current location is unknown. Salome, the daughter of Herodias, danced before her uncle, King Herod, who promised her whatever she asked; she asked for the head of John the Baptist, who had spoken against her mother (Matthew 14:3–11).

53. Jewry, the land of the Jews, Judea.

54. St. John.

On a Picture Painted by herself, representing two Nymphs of Diana's, one in a posture to Hunt, the other Bathing[55]

We are *Diana's* Virgin-Train,
Descended of no Mortal Strain;
Our Bows and Arrows are our Goods,
Our Palaces, the lofty Woods,
The Hills and Dales, at early Morn,
Resound and Echo with our Horn;
We chase the Hind[56] and Fallow-Deer,
The Wolf and Boar both dread our Spear;
In Swiftness we out-strip the Wind,
An Eye and Thought we leave behind;
We *Fauns* and Shaggy *Satyrs* awe;[57]
To *Sylvan Pow'rs*[58] we give the Law:
Whatever does provoke our Hate,
Our Javelins strike, as sure as *Fate*;
We Bathe in Springs, to cleanse the Soil,
Contracted by our eager Toil;
In which we shine like glittering Beams,
Or Chrystal in the Chrystal Streams;
Though *Venus* we transcend in Form,
No wanton Flames our Bosoms warm!
If you ask where such Wights[59] do dwell,
In what Bless't Clime, that so excel?
The Poets only that can tell.

55. A reference to a painting by Killigrew whose current location is unknown. In classical mythology, Diana, the virgin goddess of the moon, is associated with hunting; the story of Diana and her nymphs being surprised while bathing by the hunter Actaeon, whom she turns into stag, was a popular subject for Renaissance artists such as Titian and Rembrandt.

56. Female deer.

57. In classical mythology, fauns and satyrs, half-animal, half-male creatures of the woods, are associated with lust.

58. In classical mythology, spirits who haunt woods and groves.

59. An Old English word meaning a people or being (*OED*).

An Invective[60] against Gold

Of all the Poisons that the fruitful Earth
E'er yet brought forth, or Monsters she gave Birth,
Nought to Mankind has e'er so fatal been,
As thou, accursed Gold, their Care and Sin.

Methinks I the Advent'rous Merchant see,
Ploughing the faithless Seas, in search of thee,
His dearest Wife and Children left behind,
(His real Wealth) while he, a Slave to th' Wind,
Sometimes becalm'd, the Shore with longing Eyes
Wishes to see, and what he wishes, Spies:
For a rude Tempest wakes him from his Dream,
And Strands his Bark[61] by a more sad Extreme.
Thus, hopeless Wretch, is his whole Life-time spent,
And though thrice Wreck't, he's no Wiser than he went.

Again, I see, the Heavenly Fair despis'd,
A Hag like Hell, with Gold, more highly priz'd;
Men's Faith betray'd, their Prince and Country Sold,
Their God deny'd, all for the Idol Gold.

Unhappy Wretch, who first found out the Ore,
What kind of Vengeance rests for thee in store?
If *Nebat's* Son, that *Israel* led astray,[62]
Meet a severe Reward at the last Day?
Some strange unheard-of Judgment thou wilt find,
Who thus hast caus'd to Sin all Human Kind.

60. A violent verbal attack, a denunciation.

61. A small ship.

62. Jeroboam, son of Nebat, raised an alter to worship Baal with idols of young bulls, causing a division among the people of the kingdom (1 Kings 14:9–16).

The Miseries of Man

In that so temperate Soil *Arcadia*[63] nam'd,
For fertile Pasturage by Poets fam'd;
Stands a steep Hill, whose lofty jetting Crown,
Casts o'er the neighboring Plains, a seeming Frown;
Close at its mossy Foot an aged Wood,
Compos'd of various Trees, there long has stood,
Whose thick united Tops scorn the Sun's Ray,
And hardly will admit the Eye of Day.
By oblique windings through this gloomy Shade,
Has a clear purling Stream its Passage made,
The *Nymph*, as discontented seem'd t'ave chose
This sad Recess to murmur forth her Woes.

To this Retreat, urg'd by tormenting Care,
The melancholy *Cloris* did repair,
As a fit Place to take the sad Relief
Of Sighs and Tears, to ease oppressing Grief.
Near to the Mourning *Nymph* she chose a Seat,
And these Complaints did to the Shades repeat.

Ah wretched, truly wretched Human Race!
Your Woes from what Beginning shall I trace,
Where End, from your first feeble New-born Cries,
To the last Tears that wet your dying Eyes?
Man, Common Foe, assail'd on ev'ry hand,
Finds that no Ill does Neuter[64] by him stand,
Inexorable Death, Lean Poverty,
Pale Sickness, ever sad Captivity.
Can I, alas, the sev'ral Parties name,
Which, muster'd up, the Dreadful Army frame?
And sometimes in One Body all Unite,

63. In Greek mythology, Arcadia, home of the god Pan, is celebrated as an unspoiled natural landscape.

64. To stand neuter is to remain neutral or not take part; the line thus says that any ill or evil will affect the individual it touches.

Sometimes again do separately fight:
While sure Success on either Way does wait,
Either a Swift, or else a Ling'ring Fate.

But why 'gainst thee, O *Death*! should I inveigh,[65]
That to our Quiet art the only way?
And yet I would (could I thy Dart command)
Cry, Here O strike! and there O hold thy Hand!
The Lov'd, the Happy, and the Youthful spare,
And end the Sad, the Sick, the Poor Man's Care.
But whether thou or Blind, or Cruel art,
Whether 'tis Chance, or Malice, guides thy Dart,
Thou from the Parents' Arms dost pull away
The hopeful Child, their Ages only stay:
The Two, whom Friendship in dear Bands has ty'd,
Thou dost with a remorseless hand divide;
Friendship, the Cement, that does faster twine
Two Souls, than that which Soul and Body join:
Thousands have been, who their own Blood did spill,
But never any yet his Friend did kill.
Then 'gainst thy Dart what Armor can be found,
Who, where thou do'st not strike, do'st deepest wound?
Thy Pity, than thy Wrath's more bitter far,
Most cruel, where 'twould seem the most to spare:
Yet thou of many Evils art but One,
Though thou by much too many art alone.

What shall I say of *Poverty*, whence flows?
To miserable Man so many Woes?
Ridiculous Evil which too oft we prove,
Does Laughter cause, where it should Pity move;
Solitary Ill, into which no Eye,
Though ne'er so Curious, ever cares to pry,
And were there, 'mong such plenty, only One
Poor Man, he certainly would live alone.

65. Reproach or denounce.

Yet *Poverty* does leave the Man entire,
But *Sickness* nearer Mischiefs does conspire;
Invades the Body with a loath'd Embrace,
Prides both its Strength, and Beauty to deface;
Nor does its Malice in these bounds restrain,
But shakes the Throne of Sacred Wit, the Brain,
And with a ne'er enough detested Force
Reason disturbs, and turns out of its Course.[66]
Again, when Nature some Rare Piece has made,
On which her Utmost Skill she seems t'ave laid,
Polish't, adorn'd the Work with moving Grace,
And in the Beauteous Frame a Soul doth place,
So perfectly compos'd, it makes Divine
Each Motion, Word, and Look from thence does shine;
This Goodly Composition, the Delight
Of ev'ry Heart, and Joy of ev'ry sight,
Its peevish Malice has the Power to spoil,
And with a Sully'd Hand its Luster soil.
The Grief were Endless, that should all bewail,
Against whose sweet Repose thou dost prevail:
Some freeze with Agues, some with Fevers burn,
Whose Lives thou half out of their Holds dost turn;
And of whose Sufferings it may be said,
They living feel the very State o'th' Dead.
Thou in a thousand sev'ral Forms are drest,
And in them all dost Wretched Man infest.

And yet as if these Evils were too few,
Men their own Kind with hostile Arms pursue;
Not Heaven's fierce Wrath, nor yet the Hate of Hell,
Not any Plague that e'er the World befell,
Not Inundations', Famines', Fires' blind rage,
Did ever Mortals equally engage,
As Man does Man, more skilful to annoy,
Both Mischievous and Witty to destroy.
The bloody Wolf, the Wolf does not pursue;

66. Onward movement in a particular path.

The Boar, though fierce, his Tusk will not imbrue[67]
In his own Kind, Bears, not on Bears do prey:
Then art thou, Man, more savage far than they.

And now, methinks, I present do behold
The Bloody Fields that are in Fame enroll'd,
I see, I see thousands in Battle slain,
The Dead and Dying cover all the Plain,
Confused Noises hear, each way sent out,
The Vanquishts' Cries join'd with the Victor's shout;
Their Sighs and Groans who draw a painful Breath,
And feel the Pangs of slow approaching Death:
Yet happier these, far happier are the Dead;
Than who into Captivity are led:
What by their Chains, and by the Victor's Pride,
We pity these, and envy those that dy'd.
And who can say, when Thousands are betray'd,
To Widowhood, Orphans or Childless made.
Whither the Day does draw more Tears or BLOOD
A greater Crystal or a Crimson Flood.
The faithful Wife, who late her Lord did Arm,
And hop'd to shield, by holy Vows, from Harm,
Follow'd his parting-steps with Love and Care,
Sent after weeping Eyes, while he afar
Rode heated on, born by a brave Disdain,
May now go seek him, lying 'mong the Slain:
Low on the Earth she'll find his lofty Crest,
And those refulgent[68] Arms which late his Breast
Did guard, by rough Encounters broke and tore,
His Face and Hair, with Brains all clotted o'er,
And Warlike Weeds besmear'd with Dust and Gore.

"And will the Suffering World never bestow
Upon th'Accursed Causers of such Woe,
A vengeance that may parallel their Loss,

67. Stain or defile.

68. Shining, gleaming.

Fix Public Thieves and Robbers on the Cross?
Such as call Ruin, Conquest, in their Pride,
And having plagu'd Mankind, in Triumph ride.
Like that renounced[69] Murderer who stains
In these our days *Alsatia's* fertile Plains,[70]
Only to fill the future Trump[71] of Fame,
Though greater Crimes, than Glory it proclaim.
Alcides,[72] Scourge of Thieves, return to Earth,
Which uncontrolled gives such Monsters birth;
On *Scepter'd-Cacus* let thy Power be shown,
Pull him not from his Den, but from his Throne."[73]

Clouds of black Thoughts her further Speech here broke,
Her swelling Grief too great was to be spoke,
Which struggl'd long in her tormented Mind,
Till it some Vent by Sighs and Tears did find.
And when her Sorrow something was subdu'd,
She thus again her sad Complaint renewed.

"Most Wretched Man, were th'Ills I nam'd before
All which I could in thy sad State deplore,
Did Things without alone 'gainst thee prevail,
My Tongue I'd chide, that them I did bewail:
But, Shame to Reason, thou art seen to be
Unto thy self the fatal'st Enemy,

69. Disowned, rejected.

70. The ancient name for the region of Alsace in Europe, a rich and productive farmland, but also a contested border area. It was once owned by the Holy Roman Emperor, but it became part of France in 1648 as part of a treaty ending the Thirty Years' War. The region was notable for its radical Protestant strongholds, and in 1681 Strasbourg, an independent city in the region, was attacked and captured by the army of Louis XIV; during this period, the area saw many bloody skirmishes between Protestants and Catholics.

71. Trumpet.

72. Hercules.

73. In Virgil, Cacus was a monster living in the hill Aventine; he terrorized and plundered the countryside around Rome. After Cacus stole some of the cattle Hercules was taking back to Greece that he had captured when he defeated the monster Geryon, Hercules slew Cacus to retrieve them.

Within thy Breast the Greatest Plagues to bear,
First them to breed; and then to cherish there;
Unmanag'd Passions which the Reins have broke
Of Reason, and refuse to bear its Yoke.
But hurry thee, uncurb'd, from place to place,
A wild, unruly, and an Uncouth Chase.
Now cursed Gold does lead the Man astray,
False flatt'ring Honors do anon betray,
Then Beauty does as dang'rously delude,
Beauty, that vanishes, while 'tis pursu'd,
That, while we do behold it, fades away,
And even a Long Encomium[74] will not stay."

Each one of these can the Whole Man employ,
Nor knows he anger, sorrow, fear, or joy,
But what to these relate; no Thought does start
Aside, but tends to its appointed Part,
No Respite to himself from Cares he gives,
But on the Rack of Expectation lives.
If crost, the Torment cannot be exprest,
Which boils within his agitated Breast.
Music is harsh, all Mirth is an offence,
The Choicest Meats cannot delight his Sense,
Hard as the Earth he feels his Downy Bed,
His Pillow stufft with Thorns, that bears his Head,
He rolls from side to side, in vain seeks Rest;
For if sleep comes at last to the Distrest,
His Troubles then cease not to vex him too,
But Dreams present, what he does waking do.
On th'other side, if he obtains the Prey,
And Fate to his impetuous Suit gives way,
Be he or Rich, or Amorous, or Great,
He'll find this Riddle still of a Defeat,
That only Care, for Bliss, he home has brought,
Or else Contempt of what he so much sought.
So that on each Event if we reflect,

74. A formal expression of praise, a panegyric.

The Joys and Sufferings of both sides collect,
We cannot say where lies the greatest Pain,
In the fond[75] Pursuit, Loss, or Empty Gain.

And can it be, Lord of the Sea and Earth,
Off-spring of Heaven, that to thy State and Birth
Things so incompatible should be join'd,
Passions should thee confound, to Heaven assign'd?
Passions that do the Soul unguarded lay,
And to the strokes of Fortune ope' a way.
Were't not that these thy Force did from thee take,
How bold, how brave Resistance would'st thou make?
Defy the Strength and Malice of thy Foes,
Unmoved stand the World's United Blows?
For what is't, Man, unto thy Better Part,
That thou or Sick, or Poor, or Captive art?
Since no Material Stroke the Soul can feel,
The smart of Fire, or yet the Edge of Steel.
As little can it Worldly Joys partake,
Though it the Body does its Agent make,
And jointly with it Servile Labor bear,
For Things, alas, in which it cannot share.
Survey the Land and Sea by Heavens embrac't,
Thou'lt find no sweet th'Immortal Soul can taste:
Why dost thou then, O Man! thyself torment
Good here to gain, or Evils to prevent?
Who only Miserable or Happy art,
As thou neglects, or wisely act'st thy Part.

For shame then rouse thyself as from a Sleep,
The long neglected Reins let Reason keep,
The Chariot mount, and use both Lash and Bit,
Nobly resolve, and thou wilt firmly sit:
Fierce Anger, boggling Fear, Pride prancing still,
Bounds-hating Hope, Desire which nought can fill,
Are stubborn all, but thou may'st give them Law;

75. Foolish.

Th'are hard-Mouth'd Horses, but they well can draw.
Lash on, and the well-govern'd Chariot drive,
Till thou a Victor at the Goal arrive,
Where the free Soul does all her burden leave,
And Joys commensurate to herself receive.

Upon the saying that my Verses were made by another

Next Heaven my Vows to thee (O Sacred *Muse*!)
I offer'd up, nor didst thou them refuse.

O Queen of Verse, said I, if thou'lt inspire,
And warm my Soul with thy Poetic Fire,
No Love of Gold shall share with thee my Heart,
Or yet Ambition in my Breast have Part,
More Rich, more Noble I will ever hold
The *Muses's* Laurel, than a Crown of Gold.
An Undivided Sacrifice I'll lay
Upon thine Altar, Soul and Body pay;
Thou shalt my Pleasure, my Employment be,
My All I'll make a Holocaust[76] to thee.

The Deity that ever does attend
Prayers so sincere, to mine did condescend.
I writ, and the Judicious prais'd my Pen:
Could any doubt Ensuing Glory then?
What pleasing Raptures fill'd my Ravisht Sense?
How strong, how Sweet, Fame, was thy Influence?
And thine, False Hope, that to my flatter'd sight
Didst Glories represent so Near, and Bright?
By thee deceiv'd, methought, each Verdant Tree,
Apollo's transform'd *Daphne*[77] seem'd to be;
And ev'ry fresher Branch, and ev'ry Bow

76. A complete sacrifice or offering.

77. In classical mythology, Daphne was a beautiful nymph pursed by Apollo; she called for help and the river god Peneus turned her into a laurel tree.

Appear'd as Garlands to impale[78] my Brow.
The Learn'd in Love say, Thus the Winged Boy[79]
Does first approach, drest up in welcome Joy;
At first he to the Cheated Lovers' sight
Nought represents, but Rapture and Delight,
Alluring Hopes, Soft Fears, which stronger bind
Their Hearts, than when they more assurance find.

Embolden'd thus, to Fame I did commit,
(By some few hands) my most Unlucky Wit.
But, ah, the sad effects that from it came!
What ought t'have brought me Honor, brought me shame!
Like *Aesop's* Painted Jay I seem'd to all,
Adorn'd in Plumes, I not my own could call:
Rifl'd like her, each one my Feathers tore,
And, as they thought, unto the Owner bore.[80]
My Laurels thus another's Brow adorn'd,
My Numbers[81] they Admir'd, but Me they scorn'd:
Another's Brow, that had so rich a store
Of Sacred Wreathes, that circled it before;
Where mine quite lost, (like a small stream that ran
Into a Vast and Boundless Ocean)
Was swallow'd up, with what it join'd and drown'd,
And that Abyss yet no Accession found.[82]

Orinda,[83] (*Albion's*[84] and her Sex's Grace)
Ow'd not her Glory to a Beauteous Face,

78. To enclose or surround.

79. Cupid.

80. "The Jay and the Peacock" is Fable 47 in the 1666 edition of *Aesop's Fables* translated by Thomas Philipott.

81. They admired the meter and the poetic skill of the verses.

82. Having been lost in the "ocean" of another poet's works, Killigrew's poems sink from sight with no ascension or elevation to bring her fame.

83. The pen name of the very popular seventeenth-century poet Katherine Philips (1632–1664).

84. A poetic name for Great Britain.

It was her Radiant Soul that shone Within,
Which struck a Luster through her Outward Skin;
That did her Lips and Cheeks with Roses dye,
Advanc't her Height, and Sparkled in her Eye.
Nor did her Sex at all obstruct her Fame,
But higher 'mong the Stars it fixt her Name;
What she did write, not only all allow'd,
But ev'ry Laurel, to her Laurel, bow'd!

Th'Envious Age, only to Me alone,
Will not allow, what I do write, my Own,
But let 'em Rage, and 'gainst a Maid Conspire,
So Deathless Numbers from my Tuneful Lyre
Do ever flow; so *Phoebus*[85] I by thee
Divinely Inspired and possest may be;
I willingly accept *Cassandra's* Fate,[86]
To speak the Truth, although believ'd too late.

On the Birthday of Queen Catherine[87]

While yet it was the Empire of the Night,
And Stars still check'r'd Darkness with their Light,
From Temples round the cheerful Bells did ring,
But with the Peals a churlish Storm did sing.
I slumber'd; and the Heavens like things did show,
Like things which I had seen and heard below.
Playing on Harps Angels did singing fly,
But through a cloudy and a troubl'd Sky,
Some fixt a Throne, and Royal Robes display'd,

85. In classical mythology, Phoebus Apollo is the god of poetry.

86. In Greek mythology, Cassandra is the daughter of King Priam of Troy who has the gift of prophecy; when she rejected Apollo's seduction, he cursed her so that while she always prophesied truly, no one would believe her.

87. Catherine of Braganza (1638–1705), wife of King Charles II; her birthday was on November 25.

And then a Massy[88] Cross upon it laid.
I wept: and earnestly implor'd to know,
Why Royal Ensigns[89] were disposed so.
An Angel said, The Emblem thou hast seen,
Denotes the Birthday of a Saint and Queen.
Ah, Glorious Minister, I then reply'd,
Goodness and Bliss together do reside
In Heaven and thee, why then on Earth below
These two combin'd so rarely do we know?
He said, Heaven so decrees: and such a Sable Morn
Was that, in which the *Son of God* was born.
Then Mortal wipe thine Eyes, and cease to rave,
God darkn'd Heaven, when He the World did save.

To My Lord Colrane,[90] In Answer to his Complemental Verses sent me under the Name of Cleanor[91]

Long my dull *Muse* in heavy slumbers lay,
Indulging Sloth, and to soft Ease gave way,
Her Fill of Rest resolving to enjoy,
Or fancying little worthy her employ.
When Nobel *Cleanor's* obliging Strains
Her, the neglected Lyre to tune, constrains.
Confus'd at first, she rais'd her drowsy Head,

88. Of precious metals, solid and weighty.

89. Emblems associated with royalty.

90. Henry Hare, 2nd Baron Coleraine (1636–1708), a gentleman of the privy chamber for Charles II; he was an antiquarian and translator who published Giovanni Francesco Loredano's work as *The Ascents of the Soul, or, David's Mount* in 1682, although it had been in circulation in manuscript since 1665; his son Hugh was also a poet and translator. The copy of Killigrew's poems held by the Folger Shakespeare Library in Washington, D.C. and used for this edition has his bookplate.

91. As in completing or perhaps with a pun on compliment, verses that offer a flattering remark; the significance of the name Cleanor at this time is unknown.

Ponder'd awhile, then pleas'd, forsook her Bed,
Survey'd each Line with Fancy richly fraught,
Reread, and then revolv'd them in her Thought.

And can it be? she said, and can it be?
That 'mong the Great Ones I a Poet see?
The Great Ones? who their Ill-spent time divide,
'Twixt dang'rous Politics, and formal Pride,
Destructive Vice, expensive Vanity,
In worse Ways yet, if Worse there any be:
Leave to Inferiors the despised Arts,
Let their Retainers be the *Men of Parts*.[92]
But here with Wonder and with Joy I find,
I'th' Noble Born, a no less Noble Mind;
One, who on Ancestors, does not rely
For Fame, in Merit, as in Title, high!

The Severe Goddess thus approv'd the Lays:[93]
Yet too much pleas'd, alas, with her own Praise.
But to vain Pride, *My Muse*, cease to give place,
Virgil's immortal Numbers once did grace
A *Smother'd Gnat*:[94] by high Applause is shown,
If undeserv'd, the Praiser's worth alone:
Nor that you should believ't, is't always meant,
'Tis often for Instruction only sent,
To praise men to Amendment, and display,
By its Perfection, where their Weakness lay.
This Use of these Applauding Numbers make
Them for Example, not Encomium,[95] take.

92. Accomplishments.

93. Short lyric or narrative poems.

94. Virgil's short poem "The Gnat," in which a sleeping shepherd is saved from being stung by an adder when awakened by a buzzing gnat, had been translated by Edmund Spenser.

95. Elaborate expression of praise, a panegyric.

The Discontent

I.

Here take no Care, take here no Care, my *Muse*,
Nor ought of Art or Labor use:
But let thy Lines rude and unpolisht go,
Nor Equal be their Feet,[96] nor Num'rous let them flow.
The ruggeder my Measures run when read,
They'll livelier paint th'unequal Paths fond Mortals tread.
Who when th'are tempted by the smooth Ascents,
Which flatt'ring Hope presents,
Briskly they climb, and Great Things undertake;
But Fatal Voyages, alas, they make:
For 'tis not long before their Feet,
Inextricable Mazes meet,
Perplexing Doubts obstruct their Way,
Mountains withstand them of Dismay;
Or to the Brink of black Despair them lead,
Where's nought their Ruin to impede,
In vain for Aid they then to Reason call,
Their Sense dazzle, and their Heads turn round,
The sight does all their Pow'rs confound,
And headlong down the horrid Precipice they fall:
Where storms of Sighs forever blow,
Where raped streams of Tears do flow,
Which drown them in a Briny Flood.
My Muse pronounce aloud, there's nothing Good,
Nought that the World can show,
Nought that it can bestow.

II.

Not boundless Heaps of its admired Clay,
Ah, too successful to betray,
When spread in our frail Virtue's way:
For few do run with so Resolv'd a Pace,

96. Metrical units in poetry.

That for the Golden Apple will not lose the Race.[97]
And yet not all the Gold the Vain would spend,
Or greedy Avarice would wish to save;
Which on the Earth refulgent Beams doth send,
Or in the Sea has found a Grave,
Join'd in one Mass, can Bribe sufficient be,
The Body from a stern Disease to free,
Or purchase for the Mind's relief
One Moment's sweet Repose, when restless made by grief,
But what may Laughter, more than Pity, move:
When some the Price of what they Dear'st Love
Are Masters of, and hold it in their Hand,
To part with it their Hearts they can't command:
But chose to miss, what miss'd does them torment,
And that to hug, affords them no Content.
Wise Fools, to do them Right, we these must hold,
Who Love depose, and Homage pay to Gold.

III.

Nor yet, if rightly understood,
Does Grandeur carry more of Good;
To be o'th' Number of the Great enroll'd,
A Scepter o'er a Mighty Realm to hold.
For what is this?
If I not judge amiss.
But all th'Afflicted of a Land to take,
And of one single Family to make?
The Wrong'd, the Poor, th'Opprest, the Sad,
The Ruin'd, Malcontent, and Mad?
Which a great Part of ev'ry Empire frame,
And Interest in the common Father claim.
Again what is't, but always to abide
A Gazing Crowd? upon a Stage to spend

97. In Greek mythology, the huntress Atalanta refuses to marry any man unless he defeats her in a race; her suitor Hippomenes follows the advice of Aphrodite, and during the race he casts three golden apples before Atalanta on the path, causing her to stop to pick them up and lose the race.

A Life that's vain, or Evil without End?
And which is yet nor safely held, nor laid aside?
And then, if lesser Titles carry less of Care,
Yet none but Fools ambitious are to share
Such a Mock-Good, of which 'tis said, 'tis Best,
When of the least of it Men are possest.

IV.

But, O, the Laurel'd Fool! that dotes on Fame,
Whose Hope's Applause, whose Fear's to want a Name;
Who can accept for Pay
Of what he does, what others say;
Exposes now to hostile Arms his Breast,
To toilsome Study then betrays his Rest;
Now to his Soul denies a just Content,
Then forces on it what it does resent;
And all for Praise of Fools: for such are those,
Which most of the Admiring Crowd compose.
O famisht Soul, which such Thin Food can feed!
O Wretched Labor crown'd with such a Meed![98]
Too loud, O Fame! thy Trumpet is, too shrill,
To lull a Mind to Rest,
Or calm a stormy Breast,
Which asks a Music soft and still.
'Twas not *Amaleck's* vanquisht Cry,
Nor *Israel's* shout of Victory,
That could in *Saul* the rising Passion lay,
'Twas the soft strains of *David's* Lyre the Evil Spirit chased away.[99]

V.

But Friendship fain[100] would yet itself defend,
And Mighty Things it does pretend,

98. A prize given for excellence or achievement.

99. In the Bible, King Saul defeats the Amalekites but is rebuked by Samuel and told that Yahweh has rejected him; David is sent for to soothe his mind with his music (1 Samuel 16:14–23).

100. Glad or content to take a certain course of action.

To be of this Sad Journey, Life, and Bait;
The sweet Refection[101] of our toilsome State.
But though True Friendship a Rich Cordial be,
Alas, by most 'tis so allay'd,
Its Good so mixt with Ill we see,
That Dross for Gold is often paid.
And for one Grain of Friendship that is found,
Falsehood and Interest do the Mass compound,
Or coldness, worse than Steel, the Loyal heart doth wound.
Love in no Two was ever yet the same,
No Happy Two e'er felt an Equal Flame.

VI.

Is there that Earth by Human Foot ne'er prest?
That Air which never yet by Human Breast
Respir'd, did Life supply?
Oh, thither let me fly!
Where from the World at such a distance set,
All that's past, present, and to come I may forget:
The Lover's Sighs, and the Afflicted's Tears,
What e'er may wound my Eyes or Ears.
The grating Noise of Private Jars,[102]
The horrid sound of Public Wars,
Of babbling Fame the Idle Stories,
The short-liv'd Triumph's Noisy-Glories,
The Curious Nets the subtle weave,
The Word, the Look that may deceive.
No Mundane Care shall more affect my Breast,
My profound Peace shake or molest:
But *Stupor*, like to Death, my Senses bind,
That so I may anticipate that Rest,
Which only in my Grave I hope to find.

101. Refreshment.

102. Discord, conflict, disagreement.

A Pastoral Dialogue (2)

Amintor. Stay gentle Nymph, nor so solic'tous be?
To fly his sight that still would gaze on thee.
With other Swains I see thee oft converse,
Content to speak, and hear what they rehearse:
But I unhappy, when I e'er draw nigh,
Thou straight do'st leave both Place, and Company.
If this thy Flight, from fear of Harm doth flow,
Ah, sure thou little of my Heart dost know.

Alinda. What wonder, Swain, if the Pursu'd by Flight,
Seeks to avoid the close Pursuer's Sight?
And if no Cause I have to fly from thee,
Then thou hast none, why thou dost follow me.

Amintor. If to the Cause thou wilt propitious prove,
Take it at once, fair Nymph, and know 'tis Love.

Alinda. To my just Pray'r, ye favoring Gods attend,
These Vows to Heaven with equal Zeal I send,
My flocks from Wolves, my Heart from Love, defend.

Amintor. The Gods which did on thee such Charms bestow,
Ne'er meant thou shouldst to Love have prov'd a Foe,
That so Divine a Power thou shouldst defy.
Could there a Reason be, I'd ask thee, why?

Alinda. Why does *Licoris*,[103] once so bright and gay,
Pale as a Lily pine herself away?
Why does *Elvira*, ever sad, frequent
The lonely shades? Why does yon Monument
Which we upon our Left Hand do behold,
Hapless *Aminta's*[104] youthful Limbs enfold?

103. In ancient Greek, the word for twilight.

104. In Torquato Tasso's play *Aminta* (1573), set during the time of Alexander the Great, the shepherd Aminta has an unrequited passion for the nymph Silvia.

Say Shepherd, say: But if thou wilt not tell,
Damon, *Philisides*,[105] and *Strephon* well
Can speak the Cause, whose Falsehood each upbraids,
And justly me from Cruel Love dissuades.

Amintor. Hear me ye Gods. Me and my Flocks forsake,
If e'er like them my promis'd Faith I break.

Alinda. By others' sad Experience wise I'll be,

Amintor. But such thy Wisdom highly injures me:
And nought but Death can give a Remedy.
Ye Learn'd in Physick,[106] what does it avail,
That you by Art (wherein ye never fail)
Present Relief have for the Mad dog's Bite?
The Serpent's sting? the poisonous *Aconite*?[107]
While helpless Love upbraids your baffl'd skill,
And far more certain, than the rest, doth kill.

Alinda. Fond Swain, go dote upon the new blown Rose,
Whose Beauty with the Morning did disclose,
And e'er Day's King forsakes th'enlighted Earth,
Wither'd, returns from whence it took its Birth.
As much Excuse will there thy Love attend,
As what thou dost on Women's Beauty spend.

Amintor. Ah Nymph, those Charms which I in thee admire,
Can, nor before, nor with thy Life expire.
From Heaven they are, and such as ne'er can die,
But with thy Soul they will ascend the Sky!
For though my ravisht Eye beholds in Thee,
Such beauty as I can in none else see;
That Nature there alone is without blame,

105. The name of a character in Sir Philip Sidney's pastoral romance *Arcadia*, believed by some critics to represent a personal allegory for himself.

106. Medicine.

107. A type of poisonous plant, sometimes called monkshood or wolfbane, a deadly poison.

Yet did not this my faithful Heart enflame:
Nor when in Dance thou mov'st upon the Plain,
Or other Sports pursu'st among the Train
Of choicest Nymphs, where thy attractive Grace
Shows thee alone, though thousands be in place!
Yet not for these do I *Alinda* love,
Hear then what 'tis, that does my Passion move.
That Thou still Earliest at the Temple art,
And still the last that does from thence depart;
Pan's Altar is by thee the oftenest prest,
Thine's still the fairest Offering and the Best;
And all thy other Actions seem to be,
The true Result of Unfeign'd Piety;
Strict in thyself, to others Just and Mild;
Careful, nor to Deceive, nor be Beguil'd;
Wary, without the least Offense, to live,
Yet none than thee more ready to forgive!
Even on thy Beauty thou dost Fetters lay,
Least, unawares, it any should betray.
Far unlike, sure, to many of thy Sex,
Whose Pride it is, the doting World to vex;
Spreading their Universal Nets to take
Who e'er their artifice can captive make.
But thou comman'st thy Sweet, but Modest Eye,
That no Inviting Glance from thence should fly.
Beholding with a Gen'rous Disdain,
The lighter Courtships of each amorous Swain;
Knowing, true Fame, Virtue alone can give:
Nor dost thou greedily even that receive.
And what 'bove this thy Character can raise?
Thirsty of Merit, yet neglecting Praise!
While daily these Perfections I descry,
Matchless *Alinda* makes me daily die.
Thou absent, Flow'rs to me no Odors yield,
Nor find I freshness in the dewy Field;

Not *Thyrsis's* Voice, nor *Meliboeus's* Lyre,[108]
Can my Sad Heart with one Gay Thought inspire;
My thriving Flock ('mong Shepherds' Vows the Chief)
I unconcern'd behold, as they my Grief.
This I profess, if this thou not believe,
A further proof I ready am to give,
Command: there's nothing I'll not undertake,
And, thy Injunctions, Love will easy make.
Ah, if thou couldst incline a gentle Ear,
Of plighted Faith, and hated *Hymen*[109] hear;
Thou hourly then my spotless Love should'st see,
That all my Study, how to please, should be;
How to protect thee from disturbing Care,
And in thy Griefs to bear the greatest share;
Nor should a Joy, my Wary Heart surprise,
That first I read not in thy charming Eyes.

Alinda. If ever I to any do impart,
My, till this present hour, well-guarded Heart,
That Passion I have fear'd, I'll surely prove,
For one that does, like to *Amintor* love.

Amintor. Ye Gods———

Alinda. Shepherd, no more: enough it is that I,
Thus long to Love, have listn'd patiently.
Farewell: *Pan* keep thee, Swain.

Amintor. And Blessings Thee,
Rare as thy Virtues, still accompany.

108. Characters in Virgil's *Eclogues*, VII; the shepherd Thyrsis lost a singing match against Corydon witnessed by Daphnis; Meliboeus is the shepherd who narrates the account.

109. In classical mythology, the god of marriage.

A Pastoral Dialogue (3)
Meliboeus,[110] Alcippe, Asteria, Licida, Alcimedon, and Amira

Meliboeus. Welcome fair Nymphs, most welcome to this shade,
Distemp'ring Heats do now the Plains invade:
But you may sit, from Sun securely here,
If you an old man's company not fear.

Alcippe. Most Reverend Swain, far from us ever be
The imputation of such Vanity.
From Hill to Holt[111] w'ave thee unweary'd sought,
And bless the Chance that us hath hither brought.

Asteria. Fam'd *Melibœus* for thy Virtuous Lays,
If thou dost not disdain our Female Praise,
We come to sue thou would'st to us recite
One of thy Songs, which gives such high delight
To ev'ry Ear, wherein thou dost dispense
Sage Precepts cloath'd in flowing Eloquence.

Licida. Fresh Garlands we will make for thee each morn,
Thy reverend Head to shade, and to adorn;
To cooling Springs thy fainting Flock we'll guide,
All thou command'st, to do shall be our Pride.

Meliboeus. Cease, gentle Nymphs, the Willing to entreat,
To have your Wish, each needs but take a Seat.
With joy I shall my ancient Art revive,
With which, when Young, I did for Glory strive.
Nor for my Verse will I accept a Hire,
Your bare Attentions all I shall require.

Alcippe. Lo, from the Plain I see draw near a Pair
That I could wish in our Converse might share.

110. A shepherd in Virgil's *Eclogues*, VII also used by Killigrew in her poem "A Pastoral Dialogue (2)."

111. Woods.

Amira 'tis and young *Alcimedon*.

Licida. Serious Discourse industriously they shun.

Alcippe. It being yet their luck to come this way,
The Fond Ones to our Lecture we'll betray:
And though they only sought a private shade,
Perhaps they may depart more Virtuous made.
I will accost them. Gentle Nymph and Swain,
Good *Melibæus* us doth entertain
With Lays Divine: if you'll his Hearers be,
Take straight your Seats without Apology.

Alcimedon. Paying short thanks, at fair *Amira's* feet,
I'll lay me down: let her choose where 'tis meet.

Alcippe. Shepherd, behold, we all attentive sit.

Meliboeus. What shall I sing? what shall my *Muse* rehearse?
Love is a Theme well suits a Past'ral Verse,
That gen'ral Error, Universal Ill,
That Darling of our Weakness and our Will;
By which though many fall, few hold it shame;
Smile at the Fault, which they would seem to blame.
What wonder then, if those with Mischief play,
It to destruction them doth oft betray?
But by experience it is daily found,
That Love the softer Sex does sorest wound;
In Mind, as well as Body, far more weak
Than Men: therefore to them my Song shall speak,
Advising well, however it succeed:
But unto All I say, *Of Love take heed.*
So hazardous, because so hard to know
On whom they are we do our Hearts bestow;
How they will use them, or with what regard
Our Faith and high Esteem they will reward:
For few are found, that truly acted be

By Principles of Generosity.
That when they know a Virgin's Heart they've gain'd,
(And though by many Vows and Arts obtain'd)
Will think themselves oblig'd their Faith to hold
Tempted by Friends, by Interest, or by Gold.
Expect it not: most, Love their Pastime make,
Lightly they Like, and lightly they forsake;
Their Roving Humor wants but a pretence
With Oaths and what's most Sacred to dispense.
When unto such a Maid has given her Heart,
And said, *Alone my Happiness thou art,*
In thee and in thy Truth I place my Rest.
Her sad Surprise how can it be exprest,
When all on which she built her Joy she finds,
Vanish, like Clouds, disperst before the Winds;
Herself, who th'adored Idol wont to be,
A poor despis'd Idolater to see?
Regardless Tears she may profusely spend,
Unpity'd sighs her tender Breast may rend:
But the false Image she will ne'er erase,
Though far unworthy still to hold its place:
So hard it is, even Wiser grown, to take
Th'Impression out, which Fancy once did make.
Believe me Nymphs, believe my hoary[112] hairs,
Truth and Experience waits on many years.
Before the Eldest of you Light beheld,
A Nymph we had, in Beauty all excell'd,
Rodanthe[113] call'd, in whom each Grace did shine,
Could make a Mortal Maid appear Divine.
And none could say, where most her Charms did lie,
In her enchanting Tongue, or conquering Eye.
Her Virtue yet her Beauties so out-shon,
As Beauty did the Garments she put on!
Among the Swains, which here their Flocks then fed,

112. Grey or white with age.

113. In Greek myth, a beautiful nymph constantly pursued by suitors, all of whom she rejected; to rescue her, Diana turned her into a rose and her suitors into its thorns.

Alcander with the highest held his head;
The most Accomplish't was esteem'd to be,
Of comely Form, well-grac't Activity;
The *Muses* too, like him, did none inspire,
None so did stop the Pipe, or touch the Lyre;
Sweet was his Voice, and Eloquent his Tongue;
Alike admired when he Spoke, or Sung!
But these so much Excelling parts the Swain,
With Imperfections no less Great, did stain:
For proud he was, of an Ungovern'd Will,
With Love Familiar, but a Stranger still
To Faith and Constancy; and did his Heart,
Retaining none, expose to ev'ry Dart.
Hapless *Rodanthe,* the Fond Rover,[114] caught,
To whom, for Love, with usual Arts he sought;
Which she, ah too unwary, did bestow:
'Cause True herself, believ'd that he was so.
But he, alas, more wav'ring than the Wind,
Straight broke the Chain, she thought so fast did bind;
For he no sooner saw her Heart was gain'd,
But he as soon the Victory disdain'd;
Made Love else-where, as if 'twere like Renown,
Hearts to subdue, as to take in a Town:
But in the One as Manhood does prevail,
Both Truth and Manhood in the other fail.
And now the Nymph (of late so gay and bright,
The Glory of the Plains and the Delight,
Who still in Wit and Mirth all Pastimes led)
Hung like a wither'd Flow'r her drooping Head.
  I need not tell the Grief *Rodanthe* found,
How all that should assuage, enrag'd her Wound;
Her Form, her Fame, her Virtue, Riches, Wit,
Like Death's sad Weights upon her Soul did sit:
Or else like Furies stood before her Face,
Still urging and Upbraiding her Disgrace,
In that the World could yield her no Content,

114. Alcander, who is fickle in his love.

But what alone the False *Alcander* sent.
'Twas said, through just Disdain, at last she broke
The Disingenuous and Unworthy Yoke:
But this I know, her Passion held long time,
Constancy, though Unhappy, is no Crime.
  Remember when you Love, from that same hour
Your Peace you put into your Lover's Power:
From that same hour from him you Laws receive,
And as he shall ordain, you Joy, or Grieve,
Hope, Fear, Laugh, Weep; Reason aloof does stand,
Disabl'd both to Act, and to Command.
Oh Cruel Fetters! rather wish to feel,
On your soft Limbs, the Galling Weight of Steel;
Rather to bloody Wounds oppose your Breast
No Ill, by which the Body can be prest;
You will so sensible a Torment find,
As Shackles on your captivated Mind.
The Mind from Heaven its high Descent did draw,
And brooks uneasily any other Law,
Than what from Reason dictated shall be,
Reason, a kind of In-mate Deity.
Which only can adapt to ev'ry Soul
A Yoke so fit and light, that the Control
All Liberty excels; so sweet a Sway,
The same 'tis to be Happy, and Obey;
Commands so Wise and with Rewards so drest
That the according Soul replies, *I'm Blest.*
This teaches rightly how to Love and Hate,
To fear and hope by Measure and just Weight;
What Tears in Grief ought from our Eyes to flow,
What Transport in Felicity to show;
In ev'ry Passion how to steer the Will,
Tho' rude the Shock, to keep it steady still.
Oh happy Mind! what words, can speak thy Bliss,
When in a Harmony thou mov'st like this?
  Your Hearts fair Virgins keep smooth as your Brow,
Not the least Am'rous Passion there allow;

Hold not a Parley[115] with what may betray
Your inward Freedom to a Foreign Sway;
And while thus o'er yourselves you Queens remain,
Unenvy'd, o'er the World, let others reign:
The highest Joy which from Dominion flows,
Is short of what a Mind well-govern'd knows.
 Whither my *Muse*, would'st uncontrolled run?
Contend in Motion with the restless Sun?
Immortal thou, but I a mortal Sire
Exhaust my strength, and Hearers also tire.

Alcander. O Heaven-taught Bard! to Ages couldst prolong
Thy Soul-instructing, Health-infusing Song,
I with unweary'd Appetite could hear,
And wish my Senses were turn'd all to Ear.

Alcimedon. Old Man, thy frosty Precepts well betray
Thy Blood is cold, and that thy Head is grey:
Who past the Pleasure Love and Youth can give,
To spoil't in others, now dost only live.
Wouldst thou, indeed, if so thou couldst persuade,
The Fair, whose Charms have many Lovers made,
Should feel Compassion for no one they wound,
But be to all Inexorable found?

Meliboeus. Young man, if my advice thou well hadst weigh'd,
Thou would'st have found for either Sex 'twas made;
And would from Women's Beauty thee no less
Preserve, than them secure from thy Address.
But let thy Youth thy rash Reproach excuse.

Alcippe. Fairest *Amira* let him not abuse
Thy gentle Heart, by his imprinting there
His doting Maxims———But I will not fear:
For when 'gainst Love he fiercest did inveigh,
Methoughts I saw thee turn with Scorn away.

115. Speech or debate.

Amira. *Alcimedon* according to his Will
Does all my Words and Looks interpret still:
But I shall learn at length how to Disdain,
Or at the least more cunningly to feign.

Alcippe. No wonder thou *Alcimedon* art rude,
When with no Gen'rous Quality endu'd:
But hop'st by railing Words Vice to defend,
Which Fouler's made, by having such a Friend.
  Amira, thou art warn'd, wisely beware,
Leap not with Open Eyes into the Snare:
The Faith that's given to thee, was given before
To *Nais*, *Amoret*,[116] and many more:
The Perjur'd did the Gods to Witness call,
That unto each he was the only Thrall.

Asteria. Y'ave made his Cheeks with Conscious blushes glow.

Alcippe. 'Tis the best Color a False Heart can show;
And well it is with Guilt some shame remains.

Meliboeus. Haste, Shepherd, haste to cleanse away thy stains,
Let not thy Youth, of Time the goodly spring,
Neglected pass, that nothing forth it bring
But noxious Weeds: which cultivated might
Produce such Crops, as now would thee delight,
And give thee after Fame: For Virtue's Fruit
Believe it, not alone with Age does suit,
Nought adorns Youth like to a Noble Mind,
In thee this Union let *Amira* find.

Licida. O fear her not! she'll serve him in his kind.

116. Nais in Greek mythology was a water nymph; the "Virtuous Amoret" appears frequently as a character in renaissance texts, such as Edmund Spenser's *The Fairie Queene* .

Meliboeus. See how Discourse upon the Time does prey,
Those hours pass swiftest, that we talk away.
Declining *Sol* forsaken hath the Fields,
And Mountains highest Summits only gilds:
Which warns us homewards with our Flocks to make.

Alcippe. Along with thee our Thanks and Praises take.

Asteria. In which our Hearts do all in One unite,

Licida. Our Wishes too, That on thy Head may light,
What e'er the Gods as their Best Gifts bestow.

Meliboeus. Kind Nymphs on you may Equal Blessings flow.

On My Aunt Mrs. A.K. Drown'd under London-bridge, in the Queen's Barge, Anno 1641[117]

The Darling of a Father[118] Good and Wise,
The Virtue, which a Virtuous Age did prize;
The Beauty Excellent even to those were Fair,
Subscrib'd unto, by such as might compare;
The Star that 'bove her Orb did always move,
And yet the Noblest did not Hate, but Love;
And those who most upon their Title stood,
Vail'd[119] also to, because she did more Good.
To whom the Wrong'd, and Worthy did resort,
And held their Suits obtain'd, if only brought;
The highest Saint in all the Heav'n of Court.

117. Killigrew's aunt, Anne Killigrew Kirke (1607–1641), served Queen Henrietta Maria as a maid of honor, a position of significant rank and importance. Several poems (see Appendix 3) were written lamenting her loss.

118. Sir Robert Killigrew (1579–1633).

119. *Vail* used as a verb means to give a gratuity in appreciation; here, even those of the highest rank acknowledged Anne Kirke's worth.

So Noble was her Air, so Great her Mien,[120]
She seem'd a Friend, not Servant to the Queen.
To Sin, if known, she never did give way,
Vice could not Storm her, could it not betray.
When angry Heav'n extinguisht her fair Light,
It seem'd to say, *Nought's Precious in my sight;*
As I in Waves this Paragon have drown'd,
The Nation next, and King I will confound.

On a young Lady
Whose Lord was Traveling

No sooner I pronounced *Celinda's* name,
But Troops of wing'd Pow'rs did chant the same:
Not those the Poets' Bows and Arrows lend,
But such as on the Altar do attend.
Celinda nam'd, Flow'rs spring up from the Ground,
Excited merely with the Charming Sound.
Celinda, the Court's Glory, and its fear,
The gaz'd at Wonder, where she does appear.
Celinda great in Birth, greater in Mien,
Yet none so humble as this Fair One's seen.
Her Youth and Beauty justly might disdain,
But the least Pride her Glories ne'er did stain.
Celinda of each State th'ambitious Strife,
At once a Noble Virgin, and a Wife
Who, while her Gallant Lord in Foreign parts
Adorns his Youth with all accomplisht Arts,
Grows ripe at home in Virtue, more than Years,
And in each Grace a Miracle appears!
When other of her Age a madding[121] go,
To th' Park and Plays, and ev'ry public Show,
Proud from their Parents' Bondage they have broke,
Though justly freed, she still does wear the Yoke;

120. The look, manner, or bearing of a person.

121. Acting in a gallivanting, or wild way.

Preferring more her Mother's Friend to be,
Than Idol of the Town's Loose Gallantry.
On her she to the Temple does attend,
Where they their Blessed Hours both save and spend.
They Smile, they Joy, together they do Pray,
You'd think two Bodies did One Soul obey:
Like Angels thus they do reflect their Bliss,
And their bright Virtues each the other kiss.
Return young Lord, while thou abroad dost roam
The World to see, thou loosest Heaven at Home.

On The Duchess of Grafton[122]
Under the Name of Alinda,
A Song

I.

Th'ambitious Eye that seeks alone,
Where Beauties' Wonders most are shown;
Of all that bounteous Heaven displays,
Let him on bright *Alinda* gaze;
And in her high Example see,
All can admir'd, or wisht-for, be!

II.

An unmatch't Form, Mind like endow'd,
Estate, and Title great and proud;
A Charge Heaven dares to few commit,
So few, like her, can manage it;
Without all Blame or Envy bear,
The being Witty, Great and Fair!

III.

So well these Murd'ring Weapons wield,

122. Lady Isabella (1667–1723), the daughter of Henry Bennet, Earl of Arlington, who married in 1679 when she was twelve Henry Fitzroy, the 1st Duke of Grafton, the illegitimate son of Charles II and Lady Castlemaine.

As first Herself with them to shield,
Then slaughter none in proud Disport,
Destroy those she invites to Court:
Great are her Charms, but Virtue more,
She wounds no Hearts, though All adore!

IV.

'Tis Am'rous Beauty Love invites,
A Passion, like itself, excites:
The Paragon, though all admire,
Kindles in none a fond desire:
No more than those the King's Renown
And State applaud, affect his Crown.[123]

These following Fragments among many more were found among her Papers

Penelope to Ulysses[124]

Return my dearest Lord, at length return,
Let me no longer your sad absence mourn,
Ilium[125] in Dust, does no more Work afford,
No more Employment for your Wit or Sword.

Why did not the fore-seeing Gods destroy,
Helen the Firebrand both of *Greece* and *Troy*,[126]
E'er yet the Fatal Youth her Face had seen,

123. In the same way that the king's fame does not affect his power as the monarch, Isabella's beauty, although it inspires passion, does not affect her virtue.

124. In Homer's *The Odyssey*, Penelope is the wife of Odysseus (also called Ulysses in Roman myths), who is left at home when he sails to fight in the Trojan War for ten years and then is lost for a further ten years attempting to return.

125. The name of the city of Troy in Homer's epic *The Iliad*.

126. Helen was the wife of the Greek king Menelaus, who was in some versions of this story was kidnapped for her beauty by Prince Paris of Troy, although in other versions she willingly left with him, starting the Trojan War.

E'er lov'd and born away the wanton Queen?
Then had been stopt the mighty Flood of Woe,
Which now both *Greece* and *Phrygia*[127] overflow:
Then I, these many Tears, should not have shed,
Nor thou, the source of them, to War been led:
I should not then have trembled at the Fame
Of *Hector's*[128] warlike and victorious Name.

Why did I wish the Noble *Hector* Slain?
Why *Ilium* ruin'd? Rise, O rise again!
Again great City flourish from thine Urn:
For though thou'rt burn'd, my Lord does not return.
Sometimes I think, (but O most Cruel Thought)
That, for thy Absence, th'art thyself in fault:
That thou art captiv'd by some captive Dame,
Who, when thou fired'st *Troy*, did thee inflame
And now with her thou lead'st thy am'rous Life,
Forgetful, and despising of thy Wife.

An Epitaph on Herself

When I am Dead, few Friends attend my Hearse,
And for a Monument, I leave my VERSE.

An Ode

Arise my Dove, from mid'st of Pots arise,[129]
Thy sully'd Habitation leave,
To Dust no longer cleave,
Unworthy they of Heaven that will not view the Skies.

127. In Homer's *Iliad*, the kingdom of Phrygia was a close ally of the Trojans and fought against the Greeks.

128. A Trojan prince renowned for his valor in battle.

129. "Though ye have lien among the pots, yet shall ye be as the wings of a dove covered with silver, and her feathers with yellow gold" (Psalm 68:13).

Thy native Beauty re-assume,
Prune each neglected Plume,
Till more than Silver white,
Then burnisht Gold more bright,
Thus ever ready stand to take thy Eternal Flight.

II.

The Bird to whom the spacious Air was given,
As in a smooth and trackless Path to go,
A Walk which does no Limits know
Pervious[130] alone to Her and Heaven:
Should she her Airy Race forget,
On Earth affect to walk and sit;
Should she so high a Privilege neglect,
As still on Earth, to walk and sit, affect,
What could she of Wrong complain,
Who thus her Birdly Kind doth stain,
If all her Feathers molted were,
And naked she were left and bare,
The Jest and Scorn of Earth and Air?

III.

The Bird of Paradise the Soul,[131]

Extemporary Counsel given to a Young Gallant in a Frolic

As you are Young, if you'll be also Wise,
Danger with Honor court, Quarrels[132] despise;
Believe you then are truly Brave and Bold,
To Beauty when no Slave, and less to Gold;
When Virtue you dare own, not think it odd,
Or ungenteel to say, *I fear a God.*

130. Permeable.

131. This poem breaks off here.

132. In the Folger Shakespeare Library copy, this word has been emended by hand to be "but broils."

Appendix 1: Poems about Anne Killigrew

The Publisher to the Reader[133]

Reader, dost ask, What Work we here display?
What fair and Novel Piece salutes the Day?
Know, that a Virgin bright this POEM writ,
A *Grace* for Beauty, and a *Muse* for Wit!
Who, when none higher in *Love's* Courts might sway,
Despis'd the Myrtle, for the nobler Bay![134]
Nor could *Apollo* or *Minerva* tell,[135]
Whether her Pen or Pencil did excel!
But while these Pow'rs laid both to her their Claim,
Behold, a Matron of a Heavenly Frame,
Antique, but Great and Comely in her Mien,[136]
Upon whose gorgeous Robe inscrib'd was seen
Divine Virtue, took her from both away,
And thus with Anger and Disdain did say,
Of Me she Learn'd, with You she did but Play.

133. The first poem in *Poems by Mrs. Anne Killigrew* (1686), sig. a1r, presumably by Samuel Lowndes, who published the volume.

134. In Greek mythology, myrtle is associated with Aphrodite, goddess of love; the bays or wreaths made of laurel were given to winners of competitions, notably poetry.

135. In Roman mythology, Apollo is god of the sun and the patron of poetry, and Minerva is the goddess of wisdom.

136. Killigrew is classical in her appearance and stately in her bearing and behavior.

To the Pious Memory
Of the Accomplisht Young Lady
Mrs. Anne Killigrew,
Excellent in the two Sister-Arts of Poesie, and Painting.
An Ode[137]

I.

Thou Youngest Virgin-Daughter of the Skies,
Made in the last Promotion of the Blest;
Whose Palms,[138] new pluckt from Paradise,
In spreading Branches more sublimely rise,
Rich with Immortal Green above the rest:
Whether, adopted to some Neighboring Star,
Thou rol'st above us, in thy wand'ring Race,
Or, in Procession fixt and regular,
Mov'd with the Heaven's Majestic Pace;
Or, call'd to more Superior Bliss,
Thou tread'st, with Seraphims, the vast Abyss:
Whatever happy Region be thy place,
Cease thy Celestial Song a little space;
(Thou wilt have Time enough for Hymns Divine,
Since Heav'n's Eternal Year is thine.)
Hear then a Mortal Muse thy Praise rehearse,
In no ignoble Verse;
But such as thy own voice did practice here,
When thy first Fruits of Poesie were giv'n;
To make thyself a welcome Inmate there:
While yet a young Probationer,[139]
And Candidate of Heav'n.

137. Second poem in *Poems by Mrs. Anne Killigrew*, sigs. a1v–b2v. "Mrs." stands for mistress, a common form of respectful address to a young unmarried woman.

138. In the Bible and in classical literature, palms are emblems of victory (see, for example, Revelation 7:9).

139. A person in training.

II.

If by Traduction[140] came thy Mind,
Our Wonder is the less to find
A Soul so charming from a Stock so good;
Thy Father was transfus'd into thy Blood:
So wert thou born into the tuneful strain,
(An early, rich, and inexhausted Vein.)
But if thy Preexisting Soul
Was form'd, at first, with Myriads more,
It did through all the Mighty Poets roll,
Who *Greek* or *Latin* Laurels wore.
And was that *Sappho*[141] last, which once it was before.
If so, then cease thy flight, *O Heav'n-born Mind*!
Thou hast no Dross to purge from thy Rich Ore:
Nor can thy Soul a fairer Mansion find,
Than was the Beauteous Frame she left behind:
Return, to fill or mend the Quire,[142] of thy Celestial kind.

III.

May we presume to say, that at thy Birth,
New joy was sprung in Heav'n, as well as here on Earth.
For sure the Milder Planets did combine
On thy Auspicious Horoscope to shine,
And ev'n the most Malicious were in Trine.[143]
Thy Brother-Angels at thy Birth
Strung each his Lyre, and tun'd it high,
That all the People of the Sky
Might know a Poetess was born on Earth.
And then if ever, Mortal Ears
Had heard the Music of the Spheres![144]
And if no clust'ring Swarm of Bees

140. Transference.

141. Celebrated poet in ancient Greece, famous for her lyric poetry.

142. Choir, or grouping.

143. Threefold, an auspicious configuration in astrology.

144. *Musica universalis*, or universal music, a harmony believed in ancient philosophy to be created by the movements of celestial bodies in relationship to each other.

On thy sweet Mouth distill'd their golden Dew,
'Twas that, such vulgar Miracles,
Heav'n had not Leisure to renew:
For all the Blest Fraternity of Love
Solemniz'd there thy Birth, and kept thy Holiday[145] above.

IV.

O Gracious God! How far have we
Prophan'd thy Heav'nly Gift of Poesy?
Made prostitute and profligate the Muse,
Debas'd to each obscene and impious use,
Whose Harmony was first ordain'd Above
For Tongues of Angels, and for Hymns of Love?
O wretched We! why were we hurry'd down
This lubric and adult'rate age,[146]
(Nay added fat Pollutions of our own)
T'increase the steaming Ordures[147] of the Stage?
What can we say t'excuse our *Second Fall*?
Let this thy *Vestal*,[148] Heav'n, atone for all!
Her *Arethusian* Stream[149] remains unsoil'd,
Unmixt with Foreign Filth, and undefil'd,
Her Wit was more than Man, her Innocence a Child!

V.

Art she had none, yet wanted None.[150]
For Nature did that Want supply,
So rich in Treasures of her Own,
She might our boasted Stores defy:
Such Noble Vigor did her Verse adorn,

145. The modernization of Dryden's "holy day" obscures the pun here.

146. *Lubric*, meaning slippery or smooth but also wanton or lewd; *adulterate*, meaning a debased mixture.

147. Excrement or dung.

148. Virgin priestess.

149. In Greek mythology, Arethusa was a nymph who was turned into a stream of water in order to remain a virgin attendant on Artemis, also known as Diana.

150. A typographical error here is corrected to "none" in the errata.

That it seem'd borrow'd, where 'twas only born.
Her Morals too were in her Bosom bred
By great Examples daily fed,
What in the best of Books, her Father's Life, she read.
And to be read herself she need not fear,
Each Test, and ev'ry Light, her Muse will bear,
Though *Epictetus* with his Lamp[151] were there.
Ev'n Love (for Love sometimes her Muse exprest)
Was but a *Lambent-flame*[152] which play'd about her Breast:
Light as the Vapors of a Morning Dream,
So cold herself, whilst she such Warmth exprest,
'Twas *Cupid* bathing in *Diana's* Stream.[153]

VI.

Born to the Spacious Empire of the *Nine*,[154]
One would have thought, she should have been content
To manage well that Mighty Government:
But what can young ambitious Souls confine?
To the next Realm she stretcht her Sway,
For *Painture*[155] near adjoining lay,
A plenteous Province, and alluring Prey.
A Chamber of Dependences[156] was fram'd,
(As Conquerors will never want Pretence,
When arm'd, to justify the Offence)
And the whole Fief, in right of Poetry she claim'd.
The Country open lay without Defense:
For Poets frequent Inroads there had made,
And perfectly could represent
The Shape, the Face, with ev'ry Lineament;

151. A Greek stoic philosopher who lived very simply, owning nothing but a lamp and a bed.

152. A flame that shines but does not burn.

153. Cupid was associated with Eros or sensual love, while Diana was the virgin goddess.

154. In classical literature, the muses.

155. Painting.

156. The *Chambres des Réunions* established in the 1680s by Louis XIV of France to justify expanding French borders; Dryden is depicting Killigrew as conquering not only poetry but also painting.

And all the large Domains which the *Dumb-sister*[157] sway'd,
All bow'd beneath her Government,
Receiv'd in Triumph wheresoe'er she went.
Her Pencil drew, what e'er her Soul design'd,
And oft the happy Draught[158] surpass'd the Image in her Mind.
The *Sylvan* Scenes of Herds and Flocks,
And fruitful Plains and barren Rocks,
Of shallow Brooks that flow'd so clear,
The Bottom did the Top appear;
Of deeper too and ampler Floods,
Which as in Mirrors, show'd the Woods;
Of lofty Trees with Sacred Shades,
And Perspectives of pleasant Glades,
Where Nymphs of brightest Form appear,
And shaggy Satyrs standing near,
Which them at once admire and fear.[159]
The Ruins too of some Majestic Piece,
Boasting the Pow'r of ancient *Rome* or *Greece*,
Whose Statues, Friezes, Columns broken lie,
And though defaced, the Wonder of the Eye,
What Nature, Art, bold Fiction e'er durst frame,
Her forming Hand gave Shape unto the Name.
So strange a Concourse ne'er was seen before,
But when the peopl'd Ark the whole Creation bore.

VII.

The Scene then chang'd, with bold Erected Look
Our Martial King[160] the Eye with Reverence strook:
For not content t'express his Outward Part,
Her hand call'd out the Image of his Heart,
His Warlike Mind, his Soul devoid of Fear,
His High-designing Thoughts, were figur'd there,

157. The muse of painting, who unlike that of poetry, does not speak.

158. Draft or sketch.

159. Possibly a reference to Killigrew's painting *Venus Attired by the Graces*, now in a private collection; reproduced on page xvii in this edition.

160. Reference to Killigrew's painting of James II, now at Winsor Castle.

As when, by Magic, Ghosts are made appear.
Our Phoenix Queen[161] was protray'd too so bright,
Beauty alone could Beauty take so right:
Her Dress, her Shape, her matchless Grace,
Were all observ'd, as well as heav'nly Face.
With such a Peerless Majesty she stands,
As in that Day she took from Sacred hands
The Crown;[162] 'mong num'rous Heroines was seen,
More yet in Beauty, than in Rank, the Queen!
Thus nothing to her *Genius* was deny'd,
But like a Ball of fire the further thrown,
Still with a greater Blaze she shone,
And her bright Soul broke out on ev'ry side.
What next she had design'd, Heaven only knows,
To such Immod'rate Growth her Conquest rose,
That Fate alone their Progress could oppose.

VIII.

Now all those Charms, that blooming Grace,
The well-proportion'd Shape, and beauteous Face,
Shall never more be seen by Mortal Eyes;
In Earth the much lamented Virgin lies!
Not Wit, nor Piety could Fate prevent;
Nor was the cruel *Destiny* content
To finish all the Murder at a Blow,
To sweep at once her Life, and Beauty too;
But, like a hardn'd Felon, took a pride
To work more Mischievously slow.
And plunder'd first, and then destroy'd.
O double Sacrilege on things Divine,
To rob the Relic, and deface the Shrine!
But thus *Orinda*[163] died:

161. Reference to Killigrew's painting of Mary of Modena, location now unknown.

162. Coronation of Mary as the queen by the archbishop of Canterbury.

163. *Orinda* was the *nom de plume* of the well-known poet Katherine Philips (1632–1664), who also died from smallpox.

Heav'n, by the same Disease, did both translate,
As equal were their Souls, so equal was their Fate.

IX.

Meantime her Warlike Brother on the Seas[164]
His waving Streamers to the Winds displays,
And vows for his Return, with vain Devotion, pays.
Ah, Generous Youth, that Wish forbear,
The Winds too soon will waft thee here!
Slack all thy Sails, and fear to come,
Alas, thou know'st not, Thou art wreck'd at home!
No more shalt thou behold thy Sister's Face,
Thou hast already had her last Embrace.
But look aloft, and if thou ken'st from far,
Among the *Pleiades*[165] a New-kindl'd Star,
If any sparkles, than the rest, more bright,
'Tis she that shines in that propitious Light.

X.

When in mid-Air, the Golden Trump shall sound,
To raise the Nations underground;
When in the Valley of *Jehoshaphat*,[166]
The Judging God shall close the Book of Fate;
And there the last Assizes[167] keep,
For those who Wake, and those who Sleep;
When rattling Bones together fly,
From the four Corners of the Sky,

164. Anne's oldest brother Henry Killigrew (c. 1652–1712) was a naval officer, the captain of the ship *Mordaunt* on a voyage to Gambia in West Africa when his sister died.

165. In astronomy, a star cluster also named the Seven Sisters.

166. A reference to the apocalypse and the Day of Atonement at the end of the world when Christ shall return to judge all as found in Joel 3:11–14, "Let the heathen be wakened, and come up to the valley of Jehoshaphat: for there will I sit to judge all the heathen round about," and 1 Corinthians 15:51–52, "Behold, I shew you a mystery; We shall not all sleep, but we shall all be changed, in a moment, in the twinkling of an eye, at the last trump: for the trumpet shall sound, and the dead shall be raised incorruptible, and we shall be changed."

167. Judicial inquest.

When Sinews o'er the Skeletons are spread,
Those cloath'd with Flesh, and Life inspires the Dead;
The Sacred Poets first shall hear the Sound,
And foremost from the Tomb shall bound:
For they are cover'd with the lightest Ground
And straight, with in-born Vigor, on the Wing,
Like mounting Larks, to the New Morning sing.
There *Thou*, Sweet Saint, before the Quire shalt go,
As Harbinger[168] of Heav'n, the Way to show,
The Way which thou so well hast learn'd below.

John Dryden

The Epitaph
Engraved on her Tomb.
P.M.S.
Annæ Killigrew,
Doctoris Killigrew Filiæ
Quæ in ipso Ætatis flore Obiit.
Junii 16.1685[169]

Heu jacet, fato victa,
Quæ stabat ubique victrix
Forma, ingenio, religione;
Plur a colleger at in se Unâ,
Quàm vel sparsa mireris in ommibus!
Talem quis pingat, nisi penicillo quod tractavit?
Aut quis canat, nisi Poëta sui similis?
Cum tanta sciret, hoc Unum ignoravit,

168. One who announces or heralds.

169. The third poem in *Poems by Mrs. Anne Killigrew*, sigs. b3r–b4r. "P.M.S." means "piis manibus sacrum," "consecrated to the blessed dead," according to G. W. Pigman III, *Grief and English Renaissance Elegy* (Cambridge: Cambridge University Press, 1985), 147. The last four lines of the title read reads, "Anne Killigrew, daughter of Dr. Killigrew, She died in the very flower of her age. June 16, 1685" (my translation). Although there is no attribution in the volume, this epitaph has commonly been attributed to her father, Henry Killigrew. The English translation follows in the volume and is also presumably his.

Quanta, nempe, effet;
Aut si norit,
Mirare Modestiam,
Tantis incorruptam dotibus.
Laudes meruisse satis illi fuit,
Has ne vel audiret, laudatores omnes fugerat,
Content a paterno Lare,
Dum & sibi Aula patebat adulatrix.
Mundum sapere an potuit,
Quæ ab infantia Christum sapuerat?
Non modo semper Virgo,
Sed & virginum Exemplar.
Gentis suæ Decus,
Ævi Splendor,
Sexus Miraculum.
Nullâ Vertute inferior cuiquam,
Cuilibet superior multâ.
Optimi Deliciæ patris,
Etiam numerosâ optimâque prole fortunatissimi:
Priorem tamen invidit nemo,
(Seu frater, seu soror)
Quin potius coluere omnes, omnibus suavem & officiosam,
Amorisque commune Vinculum & Centrum.
Vix ista credes, Hanc si nescieris;
Credet majora, qui scierit.

Abi Viator, & Plange:
Si eam plangi oporteat,
Cui, tam piè morienti,
Vel Cœlites plauserint.

The same Turned into English[170]

By Death, alas, here Conquer'd lies,
She who from All late bore the Prize
In Beauty, Wit, Virtue Divine:

170. The fourth poem in *Poems by Mrs. Anne Killigrew*, sigs. b4v–c1v.

In whom those Graces did combine,
Which we admir'd in others see,
When they but singly scatter'd be!

Who her, *so Great*, can paint beside,
The Pencil her own Hand did guide?
What Verse can celebrate her Fame,
But such as She herself did frame?

Though much Excellence she did show,
And many Qualities did know,
Yet this, alone, she could not tell,
To wit, *How much she did excel.*
Or if her Worth she rightly knew,
More to her Modesty was due,
That Parts in her no Pride could raise
Desirous still to merit Praise,
But fled, as she deserv'd, the Bays.
Contented always to retire,
Court Glory she did not admire;
Although it lay so near and fair,
Its Grace to none more open were:
But with the World how should she close,
Who *Christ* in her first Childhood chose?

So with her Parents she did live,
That they to Her did Honor give,
As she to them. In a Num'rous Race
And Virtuous, the highest Place
None envy'd her: Sisters, Brothers
Her Admirers were and Lovers:
She was to all s'obliging sweet,
All in One Love to her did meet.
A Virgin Life not only led,
But its Example might be said.
The Age's Ornament, the Name
That gave her Sex and Country Fame.

Those who her Person never knew,
Will hardly think these things are true:
But those that did, will More believe,
And higher things of her conceive.

Thy Eyes in tears now, Reader, steep:
For her if't lawful be to weep,
Whose blessed and Seraphic End
Angels in Triumph did attend.

To the Pious Memory of Mrs. Anne Killigrew.
A Pindaric

How! Poetry and Painting both in One,
Two mighty Arts so closely join'd,
Within the Limits of a Single Mind,
We must Heav'n's lavish Wonder own!
The Weaker Sex may justly boast
Their Composition now is more divine
Than Man's, in whom so many eminent Virtues shine,
And that as much of the Almighty Work they cost.
Those noble Strains that from her came,
So full of Rapture and Poetic Flame,
Do clear as mid-day Brightness Show
What Female Wit with Learning join'd can do.
Her Wond'rous Genius could not lie
In an unactive Privacy,
Could not conceal Its gen'rous Fire,
Consume and languish in a faint desire,
But broke the sacred Prison thro',
And all around the Beams did flow,
At which the World surpris'd did gaze,
With wonder struck and deep amaze;
They scarce could fancy whence they came,
But when they saw a Woman's Name,
They soon resign'd their Laurel Crown,

Threw all their Pens and useless Paper down,
And blush'd that the Weak Sex had all their Arts outdone.

II.

Till she appear'd all Poetry lay dead,
O'ercharg'd and stifled in Its Infant-Bed,
No powrful Light could Its lost youth restore,
'Twas gone too fair, could be retriev'd no more.
Th'Old Chaos so a senseless Mass did seem,
Whose diff'ring Seeds and num'rous Atoms slept,
In a confused silence kept,
Till by the force of the Almighty Beam,
That did exert Its wond'rous Light
Amidst the dreadful Shades of Night,
And pierct quite thro' Its dismal Womb,
A beauteous World, compos'd of Love, did come:
Her lasting Numbers did as pow'rful prove,
They rais'd a Glorious World of Poesie,
And mounted It on high,
Till Its bright Spires did touch the bending Sky.
So tuneful Music once did call,
And made the cap'ring Stones to move,
Charm'd by the Magic Strength of Love,
Into a comely well-proportion'd Wall.

III.

What Art and Wit conjoin'd could do,
By her own single Hand is done,
The Fam'd Apelles[171] never drew
Things half so exquisitely fair and true,
Tho' easy Fools his skill still own.
Had He with Her contemporary been,
And all her curious Well-wrought Pieces seen,
His Pencil He would quickly have resign'd,
And soon confess'd from an ingenuous Mind,
That She alone of all the World was fit

171. A celebrated painter in ancient Greece.

To portray Nature with Excess of Wit.
Poetic Soul! but who can e'er declare,
Or in agreeing Numbers tell
Thy worth that swells beyond a Miracle;
Thy Mind as glorious was and fair
As Innocence, or the bright Morning Star,
No Sullen Clouds upon thy Forehead sat,
But charming Goodness deckt thy Face,
Propitious Beauty, and delightful Grace,
And melting Eloquence upon thy Tongue did wait.
But why should I thus vainly strive
To keep thy Memory alive,
Or why should I attempt to show
Thy dazzling Glories in a strain so low?
Thy hand alone could thy own Beauties paint,
Thou Greatest Poetess, and Greater Saint!
Now nobler Themes employ thy sacred Fire,
Thy Mind's with higher thoughts possest,
A brighter Genius warms thy Breast,
And tunes loud Anthems for the Heav'nly Quire,
Thy mighty Soul clearer Ideas frames,
Paints Heav'n in thought with far more vig'rous flames
Thou see'st all Things in their own Natures true,
Which fancy us'd to give a Being to,
All Heav'n lies open to thy piercing Sight,
Free from Imposture or the least deceit;
Whilst glowing Stars do round thy Temples shine,
And circling Rainbows thy soft Neck entwine,
Thou'rt early crown'd a Prophetess divine;
'Mongst all the sparkling Train Thou shin'st most bright,
Shin'st with a double and unsully'd Light.

John Chatwin[172]

172. Oxford, Bodleian Library, MS Rawlinson Poet 94, fols. 149–52. Little is known about John Chatwin (c. 1667–after 1685) outside of the manuscript volume of verse he composed and translated c. 1682–85; he was a student of Emmanuel College, Cambridge, where he received a BA in 1685. See Margaret J. M. Ezell, *Social Authorship and the Advent of Print* (Baltimore: Johns Hopkins University Press, 1999), 31–33.

On the Death of The Truly Virtuous Mrs. Anne Killigrew, who was Related to my (Deceased) Wife[173]

I cannot Mourn thy Fate, Sweet Maid, but Joy
That Thou art gone from all this World's Annoy,
From th'hurry of this cursed Age, that draws
Heav'n's Vengeance down by th'breach of all the Laws
Of GOD, and Man: there's nothing here but Noise
And Interruption of True Peaceful Joys.
That which they Pleasure call is *Sport* for *Apes*
Which turns the *Fancy* to a thousand *Shapes*
And Wrests the *Mind* from that *Celestial Sphere*
To which Its *Nature* ever would adhere
That by a *Constant Revolution*
Its Rest and Motion ever might be ONE
That which my Mind hath ever Sought, thy Mind
Though Compast[174] with these walls of Clay did Find:
Pure Quintessential Love, Æthereal Flame,
Which Always shines, and Always is the Same:
Here's no faint trembling Flame: all Bright appears
'Tis ne'er blown out with Sighs, nor quencht with tears.
Thy Soul Enflames my Love: the Unity
I had with Her, who was Allied to Thee
Is Now made Perfect: Our Souls' Mutual Flame
Tho Higher in *Degree* in *Nature's* still the same.
Her, Thee, and All the Glorious Souls Above
I Now Enjoy, whilst in You All I Love

173. Alexander Turnbull Library, shelfmark REng KILL Poems 1686. As Richard Morton notes in his facsimile edition of Killigrew's *Poems* which includes this verse, the poem is attributed to Edmond Elys by the antiquarian Joseph Hunter, *Poems (1686)*, viii. Elys (1633x5–1708), a Church of England clergyman, published several collections of religious verse in the 1650s while a student at Oxford. It is presently unknown what relationship his wife had with the Killigrew family.

174. Encompassed, enclosed.

The Boundless Spring of Joy to Ev'ry Mind
That knows what's *Truly Fair* and Knows what's *Truly Kind.*
How have I Labor'd to Depress the Pride
Of one [Dr. Parker][175] that strives Illustrious Truth to Hide
In the *Thick Bushes of Learn'd Sophistry,*
Which he that Enters hardly sees the Sky?
Truth that thy Splendid Soul did clearly see
And of it made a plain Discovery.
And having Conquer'd Fate, Thou leav'st those Arms [Her Poems]
By which Mankind may Conquer All their Harms
And make them Serve their Noble Purposes,
All Good to Gain, All Evil to Repress.
How Bravely did thy *Melibaeus*[176] show
The Madness of that Love most men pursue
And how Youth may their strongest Lusts subdue!
O Happy Maid, who didst so soone Espy
In This *Dark Life, that All is Vanity*!
May thy Bright Love, All Youthful Minds Inspire,
And like the SUN, put out all *other Fire*;
May all the Virtuous Celebrate thy Name;
All Poets' Hearts Partake of thy Great Flame
That all their Ardors and their Flights may be
The Flames that Fly up to the *Deity*;
That DAVID's Muse they all may Imitate,
Sing Virtue's Triumphs o'er the Power of Fate:
That all their Works Resembling Heav'n may prove
The Blest Effects of Glory, Power, and Love.

E.E. 1685

175. In 1680, Elys published a rebuttal to Dr. Samuel Parker, *Epistola ad Sam. Parkerum S.T.P.*

176. Reference to the shepherd in Virgil's *Eclogues*, VII, whom Killigrew also uses in her "A Pastoral Dialogue (3)".

Anagram[177] on Mistress Anne Killigrew, who wrote one or more divine Poems[178]
My rare wit killing Sin

Rare wit, more rarely use'd, her noble aim,
Was to reform the Age, from sin reclaim;
She slighted those low ends, her own high praise;
Shouts of applause, or wreathes of verdant bays;
She virtue's cause espous'd; bold vice defied,
Her life and deathless living work its pow'r destroy'd.

Edmund Wodehouse

177. A type of word game in which the letters of one word or phrase are rearranged to make a new word or phrase; this is not an example of a perfect anagram which makes use of all the letters.

178. In the hand of Edmund Wodehouse in a large manuscript miscellany apparently begun by his father Sir Philip Wodehouse, an MP for Norfolk who served in the House of Commons during the Interregnum; little is known about his son. University of Leeds, Brotherton Collection, MS Lt 40, fol. 124v.

Appendix 2: Poems by others printed at the end of Killigrew's Poems *but not by her*

These Three following ODES being found among Mrs. Killigrew's Papers, I was willing to Print though none of hers.[179]

Cloris's Charms Dissolved by Eudora

I.

Not that thy Fair Hand
Should lead me from my deep Despair,
Or thy Love, *Cloris*, End my Care,
And back my Steps command:
But if hereafter thou Retire,
To quench with Tears, thy Wand'ring Fire,
This Clue I'll leave behind,
By which thou may'st untwine
The Saddest Way,
To shun the Day,
That ever Grief did find.

II.

First take thy Hapless Way
Along the Rocky Northern Shore,
Infamous for the Matchless Store
Of Wracks within that Bay.
None o'er the Cursed Beach e'er crost,
Unless the Robb'd, the Wrack'd, or Lost
Where on the Strand lie spread,
The Skulls of many Dead.
Their mingl'd Bones,
Among the Stones,
Thy Wretched Feet must tread.

179. This note precedes the last three poems in the original publication.

III.

The Trees along the Coast,
Stretch forth to Heaven their blasted Arms,
As if they plain'd[180] the North wind's harms,
And Youthful Verdure[181] lost.
There stands a Grove of Fatal Yew,[182]
Where Sun ne'er pierc't, nor Wind e'er blew.
In it a Brook doth fleet,
The Noise must guide thy Feet,
For there's no Light,
But all is Night,
And Darkness that you meet.

IV.

Follow th'Infernal Wave,
Until it spread into a Flood,
Poisoning the Creatures of the Wood,
There twice a day a Slave,
I know not for what Impious Thing,
Bears thence the Liquor of that Spring.
It adds to the sad Place,
To hear how at each Pace,
He curses God,
Himself, his Load,
For such his Forlorn Case.

V.

Next make no Noise, nor talk,
Until th'art past a Narrow Glade,
Where Light does only break the Shade;
'Tis a Murderer's Walk.[183]

180. Complained of.

181. Fresh greenness.

182. Yew trees were typically planted in churchyards and were associated with fables of death.

183. Supposedly a pathway where a murderer claimed his victim and his ghost now haunts the place.

Observing this thou need'st not fear,
He sleeps the Day or Wakes elsewhere.
  Though there's no Clock or Chime,
  The Hour he did his Crime,
    His Soul awakes,
    His Conscience quakes
  And warns him that's the Time.

VI.

  Thy Steps must next advance,
Where Horror, Sin, and Specters dwell,
Where the Wood's Shade seems turn'd Hell,
  Witches here Nightly Dance,
And Sprites join with them when they call,
The Murderer dares not view the Ball.
  For Snakes and Toads conspire,
  To make them up a Quire.
    And for their Light,
    And Torches bright,
  The Fiends dance all on fire.

VII.

  Press on till thou descry
Among the Trees sad, ghastly, wan,
Thin as the Shadow of a Man,
  One that does ever cry,
She is not; and she ne'er will be,
Despair and Death come swallow me,
  Leave him; and keep thy way,
  No more thou now canst stray
    Thy Feet do stand,
    In Sorrow's Land,
  Its Kingdom's every way.

VIII.

  Here Gloomy Light will show
Rear'd like a Castle to the Sky,

A Horrid Cliff there standing nigh
Shading a Creek below.
In which Recess there lies a Cave,
Dreadful as Hell, still as the Grave.
Sea-Monsters there abide,
The coming of the Tide,
No Noise is near,
To make them fear,
God-sleep might there reside.

IX.

But when the Boisterous Seas,
With Roaring Waves resumes this Cell,
You'd swear the Thunders there did dwell.
So loud he makes his Plea;
So Tempests bellow underground,
And Echoes multiply the Sound!
This is the place I chose,
Changeable like my Woes,
Now calmly Sad,
Then Raging Mad,
As move my Bitter Throes.[184]

X.

Such Dread besets this Part,
That all the Horror thou hast past,
Are but Degrees to This at last.
The sight must break thy Heart:
Here Bats and Owls that hate the Light.
Fly and enjoy Eternal Night.
Scales of Serpents, Fish-bones,
Th'Adder's Eye, and Toad-stones,[185]
Are all the Light,
Hath blest my Sight,
Since first began my Groans.

184. Violent feeling, agony of mind.

185. Stones believed to be produced by toads and sometimes worn as amulets (*OED*).

XI.

When thus I lost the Sense,
Of all the healthful World calls Bliss,
And held it Joy, those Joys to miss,
When Beauty was Offence:
Celestial Strains did read the Air,
Shaking these Mansions of Despair;
A Form Divine and bright,
Stroke Day through all that Night
As when Heav'ns Queen
In Hell was seen,
With wonder and affright!

XII.

The Monsters fled for fear,
The Terrors of the Cursed Wood
Dismantl'd were, and where they stood,
No longer did appear.
The Gentle Pow'r, which wrought this thing,
Eudora was, who thus did sing.
Dissolv'd is Cloris *spell,*
From whence thy Evils fell,
Send her this Clue,
'Tis there most due
And thy Phantastick Hell.

Upon a Little Lady
Under the Discipline[186] of an Excellent Person

I.

How comes the Day o'ercast? The Flaming Sun
Darkn'd at Noon, as if his Course were run?
He never rose more proud, more glad, more gay,
Ne'er courted *Daphne* with a brighter Ray!
And now in Clouds he wraps his Head,

186. A course of instruction to form the student in proper order and behavior.

As if not *Daphne*, but himself were dead!
And all the little Winged Troop[187]
Forbear to sing, and sit and droop;
The Flowers do languish on their Beds,
And fading hang their Mourning Heads;
The little *Cupids* discontented, show,
In Grief and Rage one breaks his Bow,
Another tears his Cheeks and Hair,
A third sits blub'ring in Despair,
Confessing though, in Love, he be,
A Powerful, Dreadful Deity,
A Child, in Wrath, can do as much as he!
Whence is this Evil hurl'd,
On all the sweetness of the World?
Among those Things with Beauty shine,
(Both Human natures, and Divine)
There was not so much sorrow spy'd,
No, not that Day the sweet *Adonis* died![188]

II.

Ambitious both to know the Ill, and to partake,
The little Weeping Gods I thus bespake.
"Ye Noblest Pow'rs and Gentlest that Above,
Govern us Men, but govern still with Love,
Vouchsafe to tell, what can that Sorrow be,
Disorders Heaven, and wounds a Deity."
My Prayer not spoken out,
One of the Winged Rout,
With Indignation great,
Sprung from his Airy-Seat,
And mounting to a Higher Cloud,
With Thunder, or a Voice as loud
Cried, "Mortal there, there seek the Grief o'th'Gods,
Where thou findst Plagues, and their revengeful Rods!"

187. Birds.

188. In Greek mythology, a beautiful young man loved by Aphrodite, who is killed by a wild boar.

And in the Instant that the Thing was meant,
He bent his Bow, his Arrow plac't, and to the mark it sent!
I follow'd with my watchful Eye,
To the Place where the Shaft did fly,
But O unheard-of Prodigy.
It was retorted back[189] again,
And he that sent it, felt the pain,
Alas! I think the little God was therewith slain!
But wanton Darts ne're pierce where Honor's found,
And those that shoot them, do their own Breasts wound.

III.

The Place from which the Arrow did return,
Swifter then sent, and with the speed did burn,
Was a Proud Pile which Marble Columns bare,
Terrac'd beneath, and open to the Air,
On either side, Cords of wove Gold did tie
A purpl'd Curtain, hanging from on high,
To clear the Prospect of the stately Bower,
And boast the Owner's Dignity and Power!
This shew'd the Scene from whence Love's grief arose,
And Heaven and Nature both did discompose,
A little Nymph whose Limbs divinely bright,
Lay like a Body of Collected Light,
But not to Love and Courtship so disclos'd,
But to the Rigour of a Dame oppos'd,
Who instant on the Fair with Words and Blows,
Now chastens Error, and now Virtue shows.

IV.

But O thou no less Blind,
Than Wild and Savage Mind,
Who Discipline dar'st name,
Thy Outrage and thy shame,
And hop'st a Radiant Crown to get
All Stars and Glory to thy Head made fit,

189. It rebounded upon the Cupid who shot the arrow.

Know that this Curse alone shall Serpent-like encircle it!
May'st thou henceforth, be ever seen to stand,
Grasping a Scourge of Vipers in thy Hand,
Thy Hand, that Furie like———But see!
By *Apollo's* Sacred Tree,
By his ever Tuneful Lyre,
And his bright Image the Eternal Fire,
Eudora's she has done this Deed
And made the World thus in its Darling bleed!
I know the Cruel Dame,
Too well instructed by my Flame!
But see her shape! But see her Face!
In her Temple such is *Diana's* Grace!
Behold her Lute upon the Pavement lies,
When Beauty's wrong'd, no wonder Music dies!

V.

What blood of *Centaurs* did thy Bosom warm,
And boil the Balsam there up to a Storm?
Nay Balsam flow'd not with so soft a Flood,
As thy Thoughts Evenly Virtuous, Mildly Good!
How could thy Skilful and Harmonious Hand,
That Rage of Seas, and People could command,
And calm Diseases with the Charming strings,
Such Discords make in the whole Name of Things?
But now I see the Root of thy Rash Pride,
Because thou didst Excel the World beside,
And it in Beauty and in Fame out-shine,
Thou would'st compare thyself to things Divine!
And 'bove thy Standard what thou there didst see,
Thou didst Condemn, because 'twas unlike thee,
And punisht in the Lady as unfit,
What Bloomings were of a Diviner Wit.
Divine she is, or else Divine must be,
A Born or else a Growing Deity!

VI.

While thus I did exclaim,
And wildly rage and blame,
Behold the *Sylvan*-Quire
Did all at one conspire,
With shrill and cheerful Throats,
T'assume their chirping Notes;
The Heav'ns refulgent[190] Eye
Dance't in the clear'd-up Sky,
And so triumphant shone,
As seven-day's Beams he had on!
The little Loves[191] burn'd with Nobler Fire,
Each chang'd his wanton Bow, and took a Lyre,
Singing chaste Airs unto the tuneful strings,
And time'd soft Music with their downy Wings.
I turn'd the little Nymph to view,
She singing and did smiling show;
Eudora led a heav'nly strain,
Her Angel's Voice did echo it again!
I then decreed no Sacrilege was wrought,
But nearer Heav'n this Piece of Heaven was brought.
She also brighter seem'd, than she had been,
Virtue darts forth a Light'ning 'bove the Skin.
Eudora also show'd as heretofore,
When her soft Graces I did first adore.
I saw, what one did *Nobly Will*,
The other *sweetly did fulfill*;
Their Actions all harmoniously did suit,
And she had only tun'd the Lady like her Lute.

190. Shining, radiant.

191. Cupids.

On the Soft and Gentle Motions of Eudora

Divine *Thalia* strike th'Harmonious Lute,
But with a Stroke so Gentle as may suit
The silent gliding of the Hours,
Or yet the calmer growth of Flowers;
Th'ascending or the falling Dew,
Which none can see, though all find true.
For thus alone,
Can be shown,
How downy, how smooth,
Eudora doth Move,
How Silken her Actions appear,
The Air of her Face,
Of a gentler Grace
Then those that do stroke the Ear.
Her Address so sweet,
So Modestly Meet,
That 'tis not the Loud though Tunable String,
Can show forth so soft, so Noiseless a Thing!
O This to express from thy Hand must fall,
Then Music's self, something more Musical.

Appendix 3: Poems on the death of Killigrew's aunt, Anne Killigrew Kirke (1607–1641)

An Elegy Upon Mrs. Kirke unfortunately drowned in Thames[192]

For all the Shipwrecks and the liquid graves
Lost men have gain'd within the furrow'd waves
The Sea hath fin'd,[193] and for our wrongs paid use
When its wrought foam a Venus did produce.[194]
  But what repair wilt thou unhappy Thames
Afford our loss? Thy dull unactive streams
Can no new beauty raise, nor yet restore
Her, who by thee was ravish from our shore:
Whose death hath stain'd the glory of thy flood
And mixt the guilty Channel with her blood.
  O Neptune![195] Was thy favor only writ
In that loose Element where thou dost sit?
That after all this time thou should'st repent
Thy fairest blessing to the Continent?
Say, what could urge this Fate? Is Thetis[196] dead,
Or Amphitrite[197] form thy wet arms fled?
Was't thou so poor in Nymphs, that thy moist love
Must be maintain'd with pensions from above?
If none of these, but that whilst thou did'st sleep
Upon thy sandy pillow in the deep,
This mischief stole upon us: May our grief

192. The river Thames, which runs through London and was used extensively for travel to and from the royal courts in the seventeenth century.

193. Exacted a fine or payment.

194. Venus is the Roman name for the Greek goddess of love, Aphrodite, who was created from sea foam.

195. In Roman mythology, the god who controls the seas, also known as Poseidon in Greek myth.

196. In Greek mythology, one of the Nereids who are beautiful women who live in the Mediterranean Sea and reside in Poseidon's or Neptune's court.

197. In Greek mythology, the queen of the sea and Neptune's wife.

Waken thy just revenge on that sly thief,
Who in thy fluid Empire without leave,
And unsuspected, durst Her Life bereave.
Henceforth invert thy order, and provide
In gentlest floods a Pilot for our guide.
Let rugged Seas be lov'd, but the Brook's smile
Shunn'd like the courtship of a Crocodile;[198]
And where the Current doth most smoothly pass
Think for Her sake that stream Death's Looking Glass.
To show us our destruction is most near
When pleasure hath begot least sense of fear.
  Else break thy forked Scepter[199] 'gainst some Rock
If thou endure a flatt'ring calm to mock
Thy far-fam'd pow'r, and violate that Law
Which keep the angry Ocean in awe.
Thy Trident will grow useless, which doth still
Wild Tempests, if thou let Tame Rivers kill.
  Meantime we owe thee nothing. Our first debt
Lies cancell'd in thy wat'ry Cabinet.[200]
We have, for Her thou sent'st us from the Main,
Return'd a Venus back to thee again.

Henry King[201]

198. The smooth water proved to be the most dangerous; the small brook in spite of appearances is more deadly than a stormy sea.

199. In art, Neptune is frequently depicted carrying a three-pronged spear called a trident, and it is a symbol of his power over the waves and water.

200. Chamber.

201. Henry King (1592–1669) was bishop of Chichester; he married a distant relative of Anne Killigrew Kirke's, Elizabeth Berkeley, and served as a royal chaplain. This elegy was published in his *Poems* (1657).

Epicedium[202]
On the beautiful Lady Mrs. A. K.
Unfortunately drowned by chance in the Thames in passing the Bridge[203]

Drown'd? and i'th'Thames? Oh how I grieve to see
Such fair streams act so foul a Tragedy!
Not all thy main[204] which twice a day doth flow,
Can wash this guilt from off thy conscious brow.
Like the Dead Sea thou look'st; whilst every wave
Thou wear'st, now seems to be another grave.
Forgetful *Lethe*,[205] or the Stygian Lake,[206]
As thou foul *Tiber*,[207] looks not half so black.
How horrid thou appear'st! and thou dost taste
Sour, and not half so pleasant as thou wast;[208]
Rome now will fear to drink thee, since thou'rt dyed
With such chaste guiltless blood, and none will ride
More on thy ruder waves, thy cruelty
Since 't would not spare so fair a Saint as she.
How I could flow with anger! Chide thee too,
But thou art innocent, as pure, I know:
'Las[209] 'twas her Fate, unhappy Destiny!
Thus to thy streams, to add more purity.
Thou'rt become white again; an Element
Fit to receive a soul so innocent;
Whose body buried in thy Chrystal tomb

202. A funeral ode or hymn.

203. Going under London Bridge.

204. The open part of the sea, which flows into the Thames at high tide.

205. In Greek mythology, the river that flows through Hades, the home of the dead; drinking its waters made people forget their pasts.

206. A reference to the river Styx which flows around Hades and must be crossed by the dead and whose name comes from the Greek word for hate. *Stygian* as an adjective refers to something impenetrably dark or gloomy and foreboding.

207. The river that runs through Rome, here referring to the Thames.

208. An archaic form of "was."

209. Alas.

Transparent lies, scorning earth's baser womb.
Gilt Tagus'[210] banks, nor the *Pectolian*[211]
Can boast such Golden treasure as you can.
Thou didst but lend her to the Earth awhile,
Though hast thy Pearl again, now Thame's smile.
'Tis fit such gems should by the maker's hands
Shine thus transplanted to their native sands.

Robert Heath[212]

On the Noble, and Much to be Lamented Mrs. Anne Kirke, wife to Mr. George Kirke, Gent. Of the Robes, and of his Majesty's Bedchamber, who was unfortunately drowned passing London Bridge, July 6, 1641 An Anniversary

Elegy I

What rumor's this, that on the tongue of fame
Flies like a prodigy? As if it came
To fright the Genius of the world with fears,
Nay change its moving essence into tears;
Now, now irrevocably flies the sound
Her sex's pride, illustrious Kirke is drown'd.
See how bright troops of virgins, who from far
Appear, resembling every one a star
Drown'd in a sea of pearl, do sadly rise
From her lov'd urn, each without their eyes,
Wept out, or there left burning as they'd lent
Those lights for tapers to her monument.

210. A river flowing through Spain and Portugal into the Atlantic; in classical poetry, writers such as Ovid in the *Amores* describe its sands as being gold-bearing.

211. The river Pactolus in Turkey in ancient times contained electrum, a natural alloy of gold and silver; in mythology King Midas was advised to wash in this river to rid himself of the gift of whatever he touched turning to gold.

212. Robert Heath (bap. 1620–1685?), a member of the Inns of Court, published this elegy in his collected poems, *Clarastella* (1650).

See how the Matrons lay their tires aside,
And only in their sorrow take a pride,
Their sorrow which now beautifully wears,
Instead of diamonds, carcanets of tears.
Where shall we find a frame so fully grac't
With virtues in so rich a body plac't?
That it was truly held the unmatched shrine
Of human beauties mingled with divine:
As if the heavens and nature did agree,
In her to fix the greatest sympathy
Could be between them; what was fair and good,
Inclusive possibly in flesh and blood,
Who with her gentle 'haviour and deport,
Did gain the love, not envy, of the Court.
And yet she fell untimely; like a rose,
Which in the morning sweetly does disclose
Its purple beauties, 'til the winds in love
Do with their frequent boisterous kisses move
Its fragrant leaves so rudely, that ere night
They wither'd fall; so she did, the delight
Of womanhood and virtue; in whose grave
Lie more than ere mortality shall have.
Again to boast, whose glories shall (when all
Her sex's Legends unapochryphal
For truth and beauty) in Fame's book be writ,
As a large preface fix' i'th' front of it.
That when posterity reads the rape has been
Acted by death on this bright Cherubin,[213]
The virgins may her annual Obit keep,
And big with noble emulation, weep
To understand their sex's richest store
Consum'd on her; Nature's become too poor
To frame her equal beauty, or display
Such art and wonder in succeeding clay.
And though this Lady fell, the spoil of fate,
Who with too rigorous haste did antedate

213. Cherubim, or an angel.

Her day of destiny, nothing could be found
Cruel enough to give that desperate wound,
But the false waves, who as they meant to enshrine
Her (whom they took for sea-born Ericine)
In watry arms, officiously did skip
With fluent motion from each lip to lip,
'Til being enamour'd on her balmy breath,
(Cruel in love) they kist her even to death;
And viewing then no more lie to remain
Like Crocodiles they wept o'er her they'd slain.

Elegy II

The year's revolv'd, and now once more is come
The day in which she suffered martyrdom,
And 'gainst the usual custom did expire
In water, holily as those the fire
Did sanctify for heaven, who us'd to take
Delight to run to the flame-bearing stake.
Had she like them been to've receiv'd her death,
Ere the weak fire by the wind's pregnant breath
Could have been blown into a flame, our eyes
Should have prevented tyrant death's surprise,
And let fall such a huge contracted tear,
Able to quench fire's element in its sphere.
This was the day, when that same subtle thief
Fate stole earth's comfort hence, and cast a grief
Perpetual as her virtues, o'er the face
O'th' mournful world, which can afford no place
For mirth or sport, 'til celebrated be
The annual requiems to *Kirke's* memory:
Which grows more precious, like rich mighty wine
By being long kept; or relics in a shrine
Preserv'd as sacred, which inviolate hold
The Charter of their fame though ne'er so old.
With what a serious grief do men relate

Losses in their particular Estate;
The toiling husbandman will many years
After rehearse unto his rustic Peers
His past misfortune, when the Summer's heat
Did blast his fruit, or mildews hop'd for wheat.
The greedy Merchant, if he do sustain
A loss by shipwreck in the flattering main,
Sighs at its memory; which does still renew
His wealth then drown'd to his vext fancy's view,
And must we not lament, are we not bound
Upon the day when glorious Kirke was drown'd;
When nature's sweetest fruit did blasted fall,
To solemnize with tears her funeral:
Yes to diffuse a deluge, that as she
By water met her pitied destiny.
That element to expiate its black crime
May spend its moisture on her dust, till time
Dissolve; and we translated to the skies,
(Where tears are wip't away from all men's eyes)
Exalted to her fellowship may be
Her blest companions i'th' felicity
She with the Saints possess; but 'til then
Her loss must be the grief of all good men.

Henry Glapthorne[214]

214. Henry Glapthorne (bap. 1610) was a poet and playwright, whose pastoral romance *Argalus and Parthenia* (1639) was a favorite of Queen Henrietta Maria and her court. These two elegies were published in *White-Hall. A Poem … with Elegies* (1643).

Appendix 4: A Sample of Contemporary Restoration Male Courtier Poems

A. John Wilmot, Earl of Rochester (1647–1680)[215]

Song of the Earl of Rochester

Tell me no more of Constancy,
The frivolous pretense
Of Cold Age, narrow Jealousy,
Disease, and want of Sense.

Let duller Fools, on whom kind chance
Some easy Heart hath thrown,
Since they no higher can advance,
Be kind to one alone.

Old men and weak, whose idle Flame
Their own defects discovers,
Since changing can but spread their shame,
Ought, to be constant Lovers.

And we, whose Hearts do justly swell
With no vainglorious pride,
Knowing, how we in Love excel,
Long, to be often tried.

Then bring my Bath, and strew my Bed,
As each kind Night returns,
I'll change a Mistress till I'm dead,
And Fate change me to Worms.

215. These short poems were widely circulated in manuscript copies and thus can be found in numerous manuscript collections; this poem first appeared in print in *A New Collection of the Choicest Songs* (1676). In modernizing Rochester's poems, I have used as my base texts those found in Harold Love's *The Works of John Wilmot, Earl of Rochester* (Oxford: Oxford University Press, 1999).

Impromptu[216] on Charles II

God bless our good and gracious King,
  Whose promise none relies on,
Who never said a foolish thing
  Nor ever did a wise one.

Impromptu on Court Personages[217]

Here's Monmouth[218] *the Witty, and* Lauderdale [219] *the Pretty,*
And Frazier[220] *that learned Physician,*
But above all the Rest, Here's the Duke[221] *for a jest,*
And the King *for a grand politician.*

Upon Betty Frazer 1677[222]

Her Father gave her Dildoes six;
Her Mother made 'em up a score;
But she Loves nought but Living pricks,
And swears by God she'll frig[223] no more.

216. A verse composed extemporaneously, an informal epigram.

217. This popular poem exists in multiple versions. The version here is as first printed in *The Agreeable Companion* (1745). See Love, 295–98.

218. James Crofts, Duke of Monmouth, Charles II's illegitimate son and in the late 1670s, the center of a political controversy to make him the successor to the throne.

219. John Maitland, 1st Duke of Lauderdale, who was considered by contemporaries to be notoriously ugly.

220. Sir Alexander Frazier (1607?–1681), the king's principal physician.

221. James, Duke of York, Charles II's younger brother and the successor to the throne.

222. Carey (Betty) Frazier was a maid of honor to Queen Catherine and the daughter of Sir Alexander Frazier, the royal physician, and his wife Mary, who was also a dresser to Queen Catherine. Carey Frazier clandestinely married Charles Mordaunt (1658?–1735), 3rd Earl of Peterborough, causing a scandal.

223. Slang term for masturbate.

The Earl of Rochester's Answer to a Paper of Verses Sent Him by L. B. Felton,[224] and taken out of the Translation of Ovid's *Epistles*, 1680[225]

What strange Surprise to meet such Words as these?
Such Terms of Horror were ne'er chose to please:
To meet, midst Pleasures of a Jovial Night,
Words that can only give amaze and fright,
No gentle thought that does to Love invite.
Were it not better far your Arms t'employ,
Grasping a Lover in pursuit of Joy,
Than handling Sword, and Pen, Weapons unfit:
Your Sex gains Conquest, by their Charms and Wit.
Of Writers slain I could with pleasure hear,
Approve of Fights, o'er-joyed to cause a Tear;
So slain, I mean, that she should soon revive,
Pleas'd in my Arms to find herself Alive.

A Dialogue Between Strephon and Daphne[226]

Strephon: Prithee now fond fool give o'er;
Since my heart is gone before
To what purpose should I stay?
Love Commands another Way.

Daphne: Perjur'd swain I knew the time
When dissembling was your Crime:

224. Lady Elizabeth (Betty) Felton, the daughter of the Earl of Suffolk, married Thomas Felton, groom of the king's bedchamber, but her promiscuous behavior before and after marriage made her the target of numerous satires.

225. A popular English translation of Ovid's *Epistles* by John Dryden and others was printed in 1680; Ovid's verse epistles from the *Heroides* tell the stories of women who have been forsaken by their lovers.

226. Attributed to Rochester by Harold Love; first published in *Poems, etc. on Several Occasions* (1691).

In pity now Employ that art
Which first betray'd to ease my heart.

Strephon: Women can with pleasure feign;
Men dissemble still with pain.
What Advantage will it prove
If I Lie who cannot Love?

Daphne: Tell me then the reason why;
Love from hearts in Love does fly;
Why the Bird will build a Nest
Where he ne'er intends to rest.

Strephon: Love like other Little boys
Cries for hearts as they for toys
Which when gained in Childish play
Wantonly are thrown away.

Daphne: Still on Wing or on his knees
Love does nothing by degrees;
Basely flying when most priz'd,
Meanly fawning[227] when despis'd,

Flatt'ring or Insulting Ever,
Generous and grateful never;
All his Joys are Fleeting dreams,
All his Woes severe Extremes.

Strephon: Nymph unjustly you inveigh:[228]
Love Like us must fate obey.
Since 'tis Nature's Law to Change,
Constancy alone is strange.

See the Heav'ns in Lightnings break,
Next in storms of Thunder speak

227. Exaggerated flattery or affection to get one's way.

228. Protest bitterly, attack with vehemence.

'Til a kind Rain from above
Makes a Calm, so 'tis in Love.

Flames begin our first address:
Like meeting Thunder we embrace.
Then you know the showers that fall
Quench the fire and quiet all.

Daphne: How should I these showers forget?
'Twas so pleasant to be Wet.
They kil'd Love I know it well:
I dy'd[229] all the while they fell.

Say at Least what Nymph it is
Rob's my breast of so much bliss.
If she is faire I shall be eas'd:
Through my Ruin, you'll be pleas'd.

Strephon: Daphne never was so fair,
Strephon scarcely so Sincere,
Gentle, Innocent and free,
Ever pleas'd with only me.

Many Charms my heart enthrall
But there's one above 'em all:
With aversion she does fly
Tedious Trading[230] constancy.

Daphne: Cruel Shepherd I submit:
Do what Love and you think fit.
Change is Fate and not design—
Say you would have still been mine.

Strephon: Nymph I can not: 'tis too true
Change has greater Charms than you.

229. Sexual climax.

230. Bargaining.

Be by my Example Wise:
Faith to pleasure sacrifice.

Daphne: Silly swain I'll have you know
'Twas my practice Long ago:
Whilst you Vainly thought me true
I was false in scorn of you.

By my tears my heart's disguise
I thy Love and thee despise.
Womankind more Joy discovers
Making Fools than keeping Lovers.

B. Anonymous

An Heroic Poem[231] (1681)

Of villain, rebels, cuckolds, pimps and spies,
Cowards and fools, and stormers of dirt pies,[232]
Bawds, panders, whores, even all that would be so,
Stale Maids of Honor that are wooed or woo,
Of scouring drunken drabs, foul, old and pocky,[233]
That cuckold king, lord, captain, knight or jockey,
I sing. Assist me, Shepherd,[234] as thou'rt true

231. Although the opening mimics the traditional start of a serious poem celebrating heroes, such as Killigrew's own "Alexandreis," in this satire, the adventures are not of heroes but instead prostitutes and politicians, making it a mock epic. The satire circulated widely in manuscript and many copies survive in manuscript miscellanies; this modernization is based on the version published in John Harold Wilson's *Court Satires of the Restoration* (Columbus: Ohio State University Press, 1976), 68–72.

232. A reference to the artificial fortifications created for a performance staged at Windsor Castle in 1678 of the military siege of Maastricht of 1673, in which Charles's illegitimate son the Duke of Monmouth established what many believe was his inflated reputation as a military commander.

233. Pock-marked, suggesting venereal disease.

234. Sir Fleetwood Shepherd (1634–1698) courtier and minor poet, who also served as the tutor to Charles II's illegitimate son with Nell Gwyn.

To sacred scandal. Aid me, Fanshaw,[235] too;
So may thy princess[236] thy King's evil cure,[237]
So may ye drink while Dorset's[238] rents endure.
    Perkin,[239] shall never I lampoon rehearse
But thou must thrust thyself into my verse?
Begone, for satire's weary of thee grown,
As thou art of the cause thou seem'st to own.
Thy chief deserts were but at best our sport,
And scandal scorns thee now as does the Court.
    But of all villains Macclesfield's[240] the worst;
The royal cause was always in him cursed.
When gallant, bare-faced rogues forsook it quite,
And openly against their king durst fight,
He was a vermin that stuck fast to bite;
Put sullen virtue on to cloak his sin,
Scipio without, but Cataline within.[241]

235. William Fanshawe, a minor courtier, married to Mary, the daughter of Charles II's first mistress, Lucy Walter, and thus half-sister to the Duke of Monmouth; Mary's father is unknown, although Charles II did give her a substantial pension.

236. Mary Fanshawe, ironically styled a princess here.

237. Satiric reference to the belief that a king could heal by touch.

238. Charles Sackville (1643–1706), Earl of Dorset, a politician, poet, and patron of writers, was a close associate of Charles II.

239. A derisive name for the Duke of Monmouth, derived from the name of Perkin Warbeck, who attempted to claim the throne from Henry VII; it was supposedly given to Monmouth by Nell Gwyn when he returned to court in 1679 against Charles II's command that he stay out of England to avoid encouraging the Whig party's attempt to block James, Duke of York from the succession.

240. Charles Gerard (1618–1694), 1st Earl of Macclesfield, who fought for the royalists in the Civil War and also served with distinction in the Dutch wars; later in politics he joined the Whig party and became a staunch foe of James, Duke of York, voting in favor of the Exclusion Bill (1680) to block James from the succession, in spite of being granted promoted to an earldom by Charles II in 1679. Described by Samuel Pepys in his diary as "a very proud and wicked man" (December 9, 1667).

241. Scipio (237–183 BC) was a Roman general who was the hero of the Punic War; Lucius Sergius Catilina (108–62 BC), a Roman politician, was a notorious conspirator who attempted to overthrow the Roman senate.

Witness against him Newark,[242] where his pride
And falsehood drew him to the rebels' side;
Unmoved, he saw's afflicted master's tears,
And heard his plaints, yet still he has his ears.[243]
A son he has too (Brandon is his name),
For playhouse noises much renowned by fame,
And midnight brawls.[244] Arms, arms is all his joy,
For 'tis recorded once he slew a boy.
This fat, unwieldy fool would needs be great,
So in the lower senate got a seat,[245]
Where in the government great faults he saw,
For from his sire he loyalty did draw,
And learned Cox the Tartar[246] taught him law.
But for a faithful friend give me Bab May,[247]
Who scorns as much to cheat as to betray,
Keeps from his master's friends his bounty close,
But lavishes his weakness to his foes;
Nay, to deserve a confidence so large,
Still keeps cast shitten Moll[248] at the King's charge.

242. Macclesfield briefly abandoned Charles I's side in 1645 when a friend of his was removed from being the governor of Newark; according to some histories, Charles I wept on seeing him leave.

243. Ear-cropping was a punishment often given for publishing libels.

244. Charles Gerard (1659–1701), Lord Brandon, the son of the Earl of Macclesfield, was a notorious rake and a passionate supporter of the Whig party; he killed a servant in a drunken fit and afterwards fled to France, but was granted a pardon to return. Complaints about drunken young aristocrats disturbing theater performances in the 1670s and 1680s were numerous.

245. Brandon was elected to Parliament twice, first in 1679 and then in 1681.

246. Captain John Cox, aka "The Tartar," was prosecuted in 1680 for the sale of a pornographic book, *The School of Venus*.

247. Baptist May (c. 1627–1693), a courtier and trusted servant of Charles II, who was the Keeper of the Privy Purse, meaning that he controlled the flow of the king's cash; he was also a lover of Charles II's mistress, the Countess of Castlemaine.

248. Mary "Moll" Davis (1651–1708), an actress who became one of Charles II's early mistresses; rumors at the time about Nell Gwyn said that she gave her rival laxatives in some sweets before one of Moll's meetings with the king, resulting in her "retirement" on a handsome pension and Gwyn's ascension to the position of royal favorite.

But prithee, Fenwick,[249] wherefore art thou grieved?
Thy wants have by preferment been relieved;
Thy lady longed and had her wished delight;
The King dubbed her a whore and thee a knight,
And none can tell which best deserved the grace:
Thy mighty courage or her lovely face.
Then for Whig Arran,[250] bless us, who can bear
That jewel hanging at a monarch's ear,
When so many old gibbets on each road
Stand empty and e'en grieve for want of load?
That shrewd, discerning youth's sent here a spy.
Oh, Hamilton,[251] how great's thy policy!
Who'd guess this son, this certain son of thine,
Were fit for less than such a deep design?
Survey his face, you politicians all,
And there behold your meditated fall;
Before him let your vanquished wisdoms bow.
Victorious dullness sits upon his brow,
And in each line of his notorious face,
As in its proper indisputed place.
In full defiance to pretense of wit,
In broad Scotch characters, Fool, Fool is writ.
At thee, old Newport,[252] who can choose but laugh,
With thy white wig, white gloves, and thy white staff?

249. Sir John Fenwick (1644–1697) was a soldier and gentleman of Charles II's privy chamber; he along with several other drunken courtiers killed a watchman outside a brothel in 1671; there were rumors that his wife Mary had been seduced by Charles II, resulting in her husband's promotion.

250. James Hamilton (1658–1712), Earl of Arran, was the son of William Hamilton (formerly Douglas), the 3rd Duke of Hamilton; this young Scottish aristocrat became a gentleman of Charles II's bedchamber in 1679, supposedly placed there by his father to be an advocate for the Scots; he was involved in numerous duels and had several illegitimate children.

251. A reference to William Hamilton, who was also called the Earl of Selkirke.

252. Francis Newport (1619–1708) was the 1st Earl of Bradford and between 1672 and 1687 was Charles's Treasurer of the Household. He was also a member of the Whig party in Parliament in opposition to the court; he was able, however, to keep his posts at court because he voted against the Exclusion Bill. His wife was Lady Diana Russell, and they had two sons, Francis and Richard.

Thou art so neat a vermin we're i'th' dark
How to divide the rascal from the spark.
But dog thou art—Pardon me, oh, you race
Of honest curs[253] if I your worth disgrace,
For you, they say, are true and never wrong
The benefactors that have fed you long.
But this vile cur's a scandal to your kind,
Who never missed the crust for which he whined;
With a she wolf of Bedford falsely joined,
And whelps begot, destined to many a kick:
Fat turnspit Frank and the starved greyhound Dick.
  Bulkeley,[254] how bear'st thee still that burden, life?
For shame, get rid of that, or of thy wife.
Was it thy choice or thy unlucky chance
To attend Godolphin's relict[255] into France?
Of fate by bullet thou hast been bereft,
But yet, what's more thy due, there's halter left.
Make that thy honorable last resort,
And come no more into the grinning Court.
  But Poslin,[256] Poslin, how hadst thou pretense
To so much roguery with so little sense?
What devil made thee dote on politics,
Hast thou a head t'riddle all their tricks?
Sure everyone that with his mother lies,
Though lewd as Oedipus is not so wise.
  Now womankind I challenge if it can
Be half so vile and scandalous as man.

253. Mongrel dogs.

254. Henry Bulkeley (c. 1641–1698) served Charles II as Master of the Household. His wife, Lady Sophia Bulkeley, served as a maid of honor to Queen Catherine and was rumored around 1680 to have had an affair with Sidney Godolphin, Lord Commissioner of the Treasury, after the death of his wife, Margaret Blagge.

255. Godolphin's rejected or cast-off mistress.

256. This nickname for one of the courtiers has not yet been tracked down. Some sources identify it as referring to Thomas Howard, second son of Henry the 6th Duke of Norfolk (1628–1684) or to Colonel Thomas Howard, the lover of the Countess of Shrewsbury. See Wilson, *Court Satires of the Restoration*, 74 n. 86 and Fergus Linnane, *The Lives of the English Rakes* (London: Piatkus Books, 2006), 75.

Crofts[257] for her sex advancing first we see,
To claim pre-eminence of infamy;
With age and ugliness and—what is worst
Of all—with sense enough to know it, cursed.
For wit she has, they say, and sure she has;
How else could she be whore with such a face?
No vulgar sense or parts of common size
To pimp for so much filthiness suffice.
She now excels in the procuring[258] trade,
The ugliest whore makes the most able bawd;[259]
For all that's learned b'experience or age,
Examples or advice of matrons sage,
Of mere necessity to her does come;
Bawding, like charity, begins at home.
From bawd to stateswoman advanced she sits
At helm and vies with any of the Chits.[260]
And who so fit for business of the nation
As those of this so public a vocation?
Bawding the mind inures[261] and does prepare
For politics as hunting does for war;
Th' intrigues and stratagems of both the same,
The like sincerity in either game.
So her the factious their chief tool create,
As Charles makes pimps his ministers of state.
    Pert Villiers, red Godolphin, widow Swan[262]

257. Catherine or Cicely Crofts (1637–1686) was maid of honor to Queen Henrietta Maria; she was the sister of William, Baron Crofts, whom Charles II had appointed to be the guardian of the Duke of Monmouth when he was a child; she lived in Whitehall on an allowance from Charles II, but she was a Whig supporter in favor of Monmouth's succession.

258. Providing attractive young women for sex to the king and courtiers.

259. A woman who keeps a brothel.

260. The "Chits" was a derisive nickname (from "children") for Sidney Godolphin, Lawrence Hyde, and Robert Spencer, Earl of Sunderland, who served as Lords of the Treasury and first Secretary of State; they formed part of the new Privy Council assembled to block the Exclusion Bill.

261. To become accustomed to or to accept something undesirable.

262. Katherine Villiers, daughter of Sir Edward Villiers, was maid of honor to Queen Catherine between 1680 and 1685; Elizabeth Godolphin was the daughter of Sir John

(For such she is since Ossory is gone,
Sacred to fame in Otway's[263] mighty line)
Shall never, never be profaned in mine;
Never till Dering[264] Villiers does embrace,
His false teeth printing in her falser face;
Till Sunderland's[265] love-cant and mien[266] prevail
That now Godolphin's[267] tender heart assail;
Till a new general[268] shall dote on Swan,
That is, till Birnam Wood reach Dunsinane.[269]
First Temple[270] shall forbear t'admire the back
Of some spread pampered stallion robed in black,
She who so long a fallow[271] land has laid,
And brought a scandal on the name of Maid,
Who while before the other nymphs she walks,
And with her hanging dugs[272] like dewlaps[273] stalks,

Godolphin and was appointed maid of honor to the queen in 1677; Cecilia Swan was a maid of honor to the queen between 1676 and 1685 for whom Thomas Butler, the Earl of Ossory, who had died in 1680, had a well-known passion.

263. Thomas Otway (1652–1685) was a dramatist and poet; he published in 1680 a long autobiographical poem *The Poet's Complaint of his Muse*, which he dedicated to Ossory.

264. Charles Dering was one of the many sons of the writer and politician Sir Edward Dering (1625–1684); a noted duelist, he would go on to become a gentleman of the Privy Chamber for King James II.

265. Robert Spencer (1641–1702), 2nd Earl of Sunderland.

266. Deportment or demeanor.

267. Elizabeth Godolphin, daughter of Sir John Godolphin.

268. Ossory served as a general in the Netherlands.

269. A reference to the witches' prophecy in Shakespeare's *Macbeth* that he should not be conquered until the forest at Birnam should move to the castle at Dunsinane, a seeming impossibility.

270. Anne and Philippa Temple served as maids of honor to the queen between 1674 and 1692; Anne also figures in the Earl of Rochester's poem "Signoir Dildo."

271. Land that has been plowed but left unplanted or unseeded.

272. A derogatory term for breasts, usually referring to the large pendulous udders of cows.

273. A long, dangling piece of skin hanging below the lower jaw of an animal such as a dog or cow.

As some milch cow that leads the tender mulls,[274]
Licks up and goads the cods[275] of slouching bulls;
So, drunk with lust, she rambles up and down
And bellows out, "I'm hulling[276] round the town."
Not Felton's wife[277] was in her youth more lewd,
Or on the rising cud has oft'ner chewed,
Nor Nell[278] so much inverted nature spewed.

274. A milch cow is a dairy cow that produces milk, having had a calf; mulls are heifers or cows that have never been bred.

275. A slang term for penis.

276. A slang term for strolling or wandering, with a suggestion of whoring around town.

277. Lady Elizabeth Felton, wife of Thomas Felton.

278. Nell Gwyn, favorite mistress of Charles II.

Bibliography

For works printed prior to 1900, the place of publication and date are given, but not the printer or publisher.

The Agreeable Companion. London, 1745.

Alexander, Julia Marciari. "Self-Fashioning and Portraits of Women at the Restoration Court: The Case of Peter Lely and Barbara Villiers, Countess of Castlemaine, 1660–1668." PhD diss., Yale University, 1999.

Backscheider, Paula R. *Eighteenth-Century Women Poets and Their Poetry.* Baltimore: Johns Hopkins University Press, 2005.

Ballard, George. *Memoirs of Several Ladies of Great Britain.* Edited by Ruth Perry. Detroit: Wayne State University Press, 1985.

Barash, Carol. *English Women's Poetry, 1649–1714: Politics, Community, and Linguistic Authority*. Oxford: Oxford University Press, 1996.

Barber, Tabitha. *Mary Beale: Portrait of a Seventeenth-Century Painter, Her Family, and Her Studio.* London: Geffrye Museum Trust, 1999.

Beal, Peter. *In Praise of Scribes: Manuscripts and Their Makers in Seventeenth-Century England.* Oxford: Oxford University Press, 1998.

Beale, Mary. London, British Library, MS Harley 6828, fols. 510r–23v.

Boswell, Eleanore. *The Restoration Court Stage (1660–1702).* New York: Barnes and Noble, 1932.

Brotton, Jerry. *The Sale of the Late King's Goods: Charles I and His Art Collection.* London: Pan Books, 2006.

Bucholz, R. O. "The Bedchamber: Grooms of the Bedchamber, 1660–1837." In *Court Officers, 1660–1837*, 20–24. Office-Holders in Modern Britain, vol. 11. London: Institute for Historical Research, 2006. *British History Online.* http://www.british-history.ac.uk/report.aspx?compid=43768.

Burnet, Gilbert. *History of my own Time.* Edited by O. Airy. 2 vols. Oxford, 1897–1900.

Calendar of State Papers, Domestic Series, of the Reign of Charles I, 1641–1643. Edited by William Douglas Hamilton. London, 1887.

Chatwin, John. "To the Pious Memory of Mrs. Anne Killigrew." Oxford, Bodleian Library, MS Rawlinson Poet 94, fols. 149–52.

Codrington, Robert, trans. *The Ten Books of Quintus Curtius Rufus: Containing, the Life and Death of Alexander the Great*. London, 1652.

Colman, George, and Bonnell Thornton, eds. *Poems by Eminent Ladies*. 2 vols. London, 1755.

Crowne, John. *Calisto, or the chaste nymph*. London, 1675.

Cust, L., and C. H. C. Baker. "Notes." *Burlington Magazine* 28, no. 153 (1915): 112–13, 116.

Dethloff, Diana. "Lely, Sir Peter (1618–1680)." In *Oxford Dictionary of National Biography*, edited by Lawrence Goldman. Oxford: Oxford University Press, 2004–. Article published May 2009. http://www.oxforddnb.com.

Doody, Margaret Anne. *The Daring Muse: Augustan Poetry Reconsidered*. Cambridge: Cambridge University Press, 1985.

Dryden, John, trans. *The Works of Virgil Containing his Pastorals, Georgics and Aeneis[sic]*. London, 1697.

Edmond, Mary. "Davenant, Sir William (1606–1668)." In *Oxford Dictionary of National Biography*, edited by Lawrence Goldman. Oxford: Oxford University Press, 2004–. Article published October 2009. http://www.oxforddnb.com.

Eliott, Brian. "'To Love Have Prov'd a Foe': Virginity, Virtue, and Love's Dangers in Anne Killigrew's Pastoral Dialogues." *Restoration: Studies in English Literary Culture, 1660–1700* 33, no. 1 (2009): 27–41.

Elys, Edmond. "On the Death of the Truly Virtuous Mrs. Anne Killigrew." Wellington, New Zealand, Alexander Turnbull Library, shelfmark REng KILL Poems 1686.

Evelyn, John. *The Diary of John Evelyn*. Edited by E. S. De Beer. 6 vols. Oxford: Clarendon Press, 1955.

______. *The Life of Margaret Godolphin*. London: Chatto and Windus, 1907.

Ezell, Margaret J. M. "Late Seventeenth-Century Women Poets and the Anxiety of Attribution." In *Women and the Poem in Seventeenth-Century England: Inheritance, Circulation, Exchange*, edited by

Susan Wiseman. Manchester: University of Manchester Press, forthcoming.

______. "Never Boring, or Imagine My Surprise: Interregnum Woman and the Culture of Reading." In *Imagining Selves: Essays in Honor of Patricia Meyer Spacks*, edited by Rivka Swenson and Elise Lauterbach, 155–69. Newark: University of Delaware Press, 2008.

______. "The Posthumous Publication of Women's Manuscripts and the History of Authorship." In *Women's Writing and the Circulation of Ideas: Manuscript Publication in England, 1550–1800*, edited by George Justice and Nathan Tinker, 121–36. Cambridge: Cambridge University Press, 2002.

______. *Social Authorship and the Advent of Print*. Baltimore: Johns Hopkins University Press, 1999.

Finch, Anne. *The Poems of Anne, Countess of Winchilsea*. Edited by Myra Reynolds. Chicago: University of Chicago Press, 1903.

Gillespie, Stuart. "Another Pindaric Ode 'To the Pious Memory of Mrs. Anne Killigrew.'" *Restoration: Studies in English Literary Culture, 1660–1700* 20 (1996): 31–35.

Glapthorne, Henry. *White-Hall. A Poem ... with Elegies*. London, 1643.

Greer, Germaine. *The Obstacle Race*. London: Picador, 1979.

Hageman, Elizabeth H., and Andrea Sununu. "'More Copies of It Abroad than I Could Have Imagin'd': Further Manuscript Texts of Katherine Philips, 'The Matchless Orinda.'" *English Manuscript Studies, 1100–1700* 5 (1995): 127–69.

Hamilton, Anthony. *Memoirs of Count Grammont*. Edited by Gordon Goodwin. 2 vols. Edinburgh: John Grant, 1908.

Harbage, Alfred. *Thomas Killigrew, Cavalier Dramatist, 1612–83*. Philadelphia: University of Pennsylvania Press, 1930.

Harris, Frances. *Transformations of Love: The Friendship of John Evelyn and Margaret Godolphin*. London: Oxford University Press, 2002.

Heath, Robert. *Clarastella*. London, 1650.

Hertfordshire County Council. "Marriages and Marriage Licenses (1538–1922)." *Hertfordshire Names Online*. https://www.herts-direct.org/ufs.

Hopkins, David. "Killigrew, Anne (1660–1685)." In *Oxford Dictionary of National Biography*, edited by Lawrence Goldman. Oxford:

Oxford University Press, 2004–. http://www.oxforddnb.com/view/article/15530.

Howe, Elizabeth. *The First English Actresses: Women and Drama, 1660–1700.* Cambridge: Cambridge University Press, 1992.

Huygens, Constantijn. *De briefwisseling van Constantijn Huygens, 1608–1687.* Edited by E. C. M. Huysman. *Historici.nl: Vindplaats voor de geschiedenis van Nederland.* http://www.historici.nl/Onderzoek/Projecten/Huygens.

Johnson, James William. *A Profane Wit: The Life of John Wilmot, Earl of Rochester.* Rochester, NY: University of Rochester Press, 2004.

Kenyon, John. *The Popish Plot.* London: Heinemann, 1972.

Killigrew, Anne. *Anne Killigrew.* Introduction by Patricia Hoffmann. The Early Modern Englishwoman: A Facsimile Library of Essential Works, Series 2, Published Writings, 1641–1700, pt. 2, vol. 5. Aldershot,UK: Ashgate Publishing, 2003.

______. *Poems.* London, 1686.

______. *Poems (1686).* Introduction by Richard Morton. Gainesville, FL: Scholars' Facsimiles and Reprints, 1967.

______. Five Poems. London, British Library, Add. MS 78233, fols. 128r–30v.

Killigrew, Henry. *Innocui Sales. A Collection of New Epigrams.* London, 1694.

______. *Sermons Preached Partly before His Majesty at White-Hall.* London, 1685.

Killigrew, William. *Four New Plays viz: The seege of Urbin, Selindra, Love and friendship, Tragy-comedies, Pandora, a comedy.* Oxford, 1666.

______. *Mid-night Thoughts, Writ, as Some Think, by a London-Whigg, or, a Westminster-Tory, Others Think by a Quaker, or, a Jesuit.* London, 1682.

King, Henry. *Poems.* London, 1657.

Laughton, J. K. "Killigrew, Henry (c.1652–1712)." Revised by J. D. Davies. In *Oxford Dictionary of National Biography,* edited by Lawrence Goldman. Oxford: Oxford University Press, 2004–. Article published May 2010. http://www.oxforddnb.com.

Lee, Maurice, Jr. *The Heiresses of Buccleuch: Marriage, Money, and Politics in Seventeenth-Century Britain*. East Linton, Scotland: Tuckwell Press, 1996.

Linnane, Fergus. *The Lives of the English Rakes*. London: Piatkus Books, 2006.

Love, Harold. *Scribal Publication in Seventeenth-Century England*. Oxford: Oxford University Press, 1993.

MacLeod, Catharine. "'Good but not Like': Peter Lely, Portrait Practice, and the Creation of a Court Look." In *Painted Ladies: Women at the Court of Charles II*, edited by Catharine MacLeod and Julia Marciari Alexander, 50–61. London: National Portrait Gallery, 2001.

Maguire, Nancy Klein. *Regicide and Restoration: English Tragicomedy, 1660–1671*. Cambridge: Cambridge University Press, 1992.

Masson, Flora. *Robert Boyle: A Biography*. London: Constable, 1914.

McManus, Clare. "Women and English Renaissance Drama: Making and Unmaking 'The All-Male Stage.'" *Literature Compass* 4, no. 3 (2007): 784–96.

Melville, Lewis. *The Windsor Beauties: Ladies of the Court of Charles II*. Revised edition. Ann Arbor, MI: Victorian Heritage Press, 2005.

Miller, John. "Anne, Duchess of York (1637–1671)." In *Oxford Dictionary of National Biography*, edited by Lawrence Goldman. Oxford: Oxford University Press, 2004–. Article published January 2008. http://www.oxforddnb.com.

______. *Popery and Politics in England, 1660–1668*. Cambridge: Cambridge University Press, 1973.

Motten, J. P. Vander. "Killigrew, Henry (1613–1700)." In *Oxford Dictionary of National Biography*, edited by Lawrence Goldman. Oxford: Oxford University Press, 2004–. Article published January 2008. http://www.oxforddnb.com.

______. *Sir William Killigrew (1606–1695): His Life and Dramatic Works*. Ghent: Rijksuniversiteit te Gent, 1980.

______. "Thomas Killigrew's 'Lost Years,' 1655–1660." *Neophilologus* 82, no. 2 (1998): 311–34.

Nussbaum, Felicity. "Actresses and the Economics of Celebrity, 1700–1800." In *Theatre and Celebrity in Britain, 1660–2000*, edited by Mary Luckhurst and Jane Moody, 148–68. Basingstoke, UK: Palgrave Macmillan, 2005.

Ovid's Epistles Translated by Several Hands. London, 1680.

Page, William. "Wheathampstead with Harpenden: Churches and Charities." In *The Victoria History of the County of Hertford*, vol. 2, 309–14. London: A. Constable, 1908. *British History Online.* http://www.british-history.ac.uk/report.aspx?compid=43283&strquery=wheathampstead.

Pepys, Samuel. *The Diary of Samuel Pepys.* Edited by Phil Gyford, based on Henry B. Wheatley, ed., *The Diary of Samuel Pepys*, 9 vols. London, 1893. http://www.pepysdiary.com.

Pigman III, G. W. *Grief and English Renaissance Elegy.* Cambridge: Cambridge University Press, 1985.

Pinto, V. de Sola. *Sir Charles Sedley, 1639–1701: A Study in the Life and Literature of the Restoration*. London: Constable, 1927.

Poems, etc. on Several Occasions. London,1691.

Reeve, Christopher. "Beale, Mary (bap. 1633, d. 1699)." In *Oxford Dictionary of National Biography*, edited by Lawrence Goldman. Oxford: Oxford University Press, 2004–. Article published October 2008. http://www.oxforddnb.com.

Register of the Chapel of St. John the Baptist, the Savoy. London, Office of the Duchy of Lancaster, Royal Chapel of the Savoy Archive.

Rex, Michael. "The Heroines' Revolt: English Women Writing Epic Poetry, 1654–1789." PhD diss., Wayne State University, 1998.

Rich, Mary. *The Autobiography of Mary Countess of Warwick.* Edited by T. Crofton Croker. London, 1848.

Scott-Baumann, Elizabeth. "'Shifting dress': The Commonplacing of Katherine Philips's Poetry." Paper presented at Warwick University Symposium "Female Commonplace Books and Miscellanies," July 22, 2011.

Shakespeare, William. *Mr. William Shakespeares Comedies, Histories, and Tragedies.* London, 1632. Washington, D.C., Folger Shakespeare Library, shelfmark STC 22274, Fo. 2 no 31.

Somerset, Anne. *Ladies in Waiting from the Tudors to the Present Day.* London: Weidenfeld and Nicolson, 1984.

Sorbière, Samuel de. *A Voyage to England, Containing many Things relating to the State of Learning, Religion, and other Curiosities of that Kingdom.* London, 1709.

Stern, Derek Vincent. *A Hertfordshire Demesne of Westminster Abbey: Profits, Productivity, and Weather.* Hatfield, UK: University of Hertfordshire Press, 2001.

Thurley, Simon. *Whitehall Palace: An Architectural History of the Royal Apartments, 1240–1698.* New Haven, CT: Yale University Press, 1999.

Vélez-Núñez, Rafael. "Broken Emblems: Anne Killigrew's Pictorial Poetry." In *Re-Shaping the Genres: Restoration Women Writers*, edited by Zenón Luis-Martinez and Jorge Figueroa-Dorrego, 49–66. Berne: Peter Lang, 2003.

Vertue, George. *Notebooks.* Edited by K. Esdaile and H. M. Hake. 6 vols. Walpole Society, vols. 18, 20, 22, 24, 26, 30. Oxford: Clarendon Press, 1930–55.

Walsh, Elizabeth, and Richard Jeffree. *The Excellent Mrs. Mary Beale.* London: Inner London Education Authority, 1975.

Webster, Jeremy. *Performing Libertinism in Charles II's Court: Politics, Drama, Sexuality.* London: Palgrave Macmillan, 2005.

Wilmot, John. *The Works of John Wilmot, Earl of Rochester.* Edited by Harold Love. Oxford: Oxford University Press, 1999.

Wilson, Derek. *All the King's Women: Love, Sex, and Politics in the Life of Charles II.* London: Hutchinson, 2003.

Wilson, John Harold, ed. *Court Satires of the Restoration.* Columbus: Ohio State University Press, 1976.

______. *The Court Wits of the Restoration.* Princeton: Princeton University Press, 1948.

______. *A Rake and His Times: George Villiers, 2nd Duke of Buckingham.* New York: Farrar, Straus and Young, 1954.

Wodehouse, Edmund. "Anagram on Mistress Anne Killigrew." University of Leeds, Brotherton Library, MS Lt 40, fol. 124v.

Wood, Anthony à. *Athenae Oxonienses.* Revised edition. Edited by P. Bliss, 4 vols. London, 1813–20.

Index of First Lines of Poems

Index